AUDITING RESEARCH MONOGRAPH

4

THE MARKET FOR COMPILATION, REVIEW, AND AUDIT SERVICES

by Jerry L. Arnold, CPA, Ph.D.
University of Southern California

and

Michael A. Diamond, CPA, Ph.D.
California State University, Los Angeles

Sponsored by
Fox & Co.

Published by the
American Institute of
Certified Public Accountants, Inc.
1211 Avenue of the Americas
New York, N.Y. 10036

To
WILLIAM R. GREGORY
Whose service to the accounting
profession will long be remembered

Foreword

This is the fourth publication in the Auditing Research Monograph series. The series, published by the Auditing Standards Division of the American Institute of Certified Public Accountants, was undertaken in the belief that research is helpful in approaching and solving significant practice problems related to the assurance function.

One of the primary objectives behind publishing Auditing Research Monograph 4 is to stimulate additional research in the compilation and review (limited assurance) area. *The Market for Compilation, Review, and Audit Services* is a descriptive, exploratory study that should encourage needed research. I believe that the study is a valuable contribution to the accounting profession.

This monograph has been designed for banker and CPA audiences. For readers with limited time to devote to the monograph, we have included a "Highlights" section.

New York, N.Y. DAN M. GUY
December 1981 Director of Auditing Research

Preface

The introduction of compilation and review services was a dramatic move by the accounting profession to expand services available to nonpublic companies. We undertook this study in an effort to examine the impact of these services on the practice of accounting. We hope that the results that follow assist the accounting profession and financial statement users in successfully implementing compilation and review services.

We would like to express our appreciation to Fox & Co. for their continuing, unqualified support from inception to completion of this project. Specifically, we wish to thank Bill Dent, Earle King, Richard Moore, and Richard Purcell for their efforts. In addition, we would like to acknowledge the contributions of Jack Farrell of Price Waterhouse, Jerry Weisstein of Imperial Bank, George Dennis of Manufacturers Hanover Trust Company, Doyle Williams of the University of Southern California, and the special efforts of Earl Keller of the University of Michigan. We especially would like to thank the study participants for their timely and thoughtful responses. Finally, we would like to thank our assistants, Mark Hoffman of the University of Southern California and Sumi Kuramoto and Tova Shifberg of California State University, Los Angeles.

JERRY L. ARNOLD, Los Angeles, California
MICHAEL A. DIAMOND, Los Angeles, California

Contents

Highlights

The following highlights summarize by chapter the major issues and findings of this study. This section is presented to allow readers to gain an overview of the study and to focus their attention on chapters of particular interest.

Chapter 1: Introduction and Background

Statement on Standards for Accounting and Review Services (SSARS) 1, which was adopted by the AICPA in December 1978 and took effect in July 1979, introduced two new reporting services—compilation and review—for nonpublic companies. These services replace the unaudited disclaimer.

This study was undertaken to address the experiences, reactions, and attitudes of CPAs and bankers concerning the services now available for nonpublic companies: compilation, review, and audit.

The six main research questions are

1. What are the actual and the projected shifts from audits to reviews or compilations?

2. What are the actual and the projected shifts from previous unaudited services to compilations, reviews, or audits?

3. What factors influence the selection of services?

4. What are the relative costs of compilations, reviews, and audits?

5. What are lenders' perceptions of appropriate conditions for compilations, reviews, and audits?

6. What are the overall attitudes of CPAs and bankers toward compilations, reviews, and audits and the role of the various services in personal financial statements?

Chapter 2: Research Methodology

CPAs from both national and local firms and bankers were selected from New York, Paterson, Atlanta, Charlotte, Kansas City, Topeka/Lawrence, Los Angeles, and Fresno. Each participant completed a questionnaire addressing the study issues. The questionnaires were completed by 138 bankers, representing a response rate of 58 percent, and 213 CPAs, representing a response rate of 61 percent. Specific questions elicited factual, predictive, and attitudinal responses. (See Appendixes A, B, and C for copies of the various questionnaires.)

Appropriate parametric and nonparametric statistical techniques were utilized to analyze the data.

Chapter 3: Study Results—CPAs

There was very slight movement (2.5 percent) away from audits to reviews or compilations.

Forty percent of companies that previously had received unaudited disclaimers were receiving some assurance in the form of audits or reviews.

Perceived needs of outside users, the client's system of internal control, and prior experience with the client are the dominant factors influencing CPAs in their recommendations for a given level of service.

For a new client, a compilation requires 20 to 25 percent of the hours required for an audit, and a review requires 49 percent. For a continuing client, a review requires 44 percent of the hours needed for an audit.

Most CPAs feel that the adoption of SSARS 1 represented a positive development by the accounting profession.

The minimum level of service appropriate for business clients is a compilation with disclosures or a review. For personal financial statements a compilation is acceptable.

Chapter 4: Study Results—Bankers

Approximately 20 percent of customers furnishing audited financial statements prior to SSARS 1 have moved to reviews or compilations. The difference from the CPA estimate (2.5 percent) is explained by the experiences of a minority of bankers, who have encountered substantial movement away from audit.

Approximately 8 percent of the customers previously furnishing unaudited financial statements now are audited.

Traditional lending factors, including loan size and the customer's capital structure, have the greatest influence on the banker's decision to require a given level of service. Relative costs of the services are least important.

Bankers tend to feel that introduction of compilation and review services represented a positive development by the accounting profession.

The required level of service increases commensurately with the size and complexity of the loan. For personal financial statements a compilation is most appropriate.

Chapter 5: Summary and Recommendations

- The accounting profession should continue to study the levels of service appropriate for nonpublic companies.

- Accountants should make an effort to determine the attitudes of their clients' bankers toward compilations, reviews, and audits.

- The accounting profession should increase CPAs' awareness that use of the unaudited disclaimer for nonpublic companies is prohibited.

- The accounting profession should take steps to ensure that the unaudited disclaimer is no longer used, and corrective action should be taken where appropriate.

- Consideration should be given to prohibiting the use of the "unaudited" stamp on financial statements.

- Bankers should be educated about the differences between the unaudited services currently and previously available.

- Both formal and informal interactions between CPAs and bankers should increase, with both groups sharing their perspectives and expertise.

- Future SSARS pronouncements should be structured in a manner similar to the existing ones.

1

Introduction and Background

Until July 1979 CPAs were permitted either to audit a nonpublic company's financial statements and express an appropriate audit opinion or to disclaim an opinion if the statements were not audited. On July 1, 1979, Statement on Standards for Accounting and Review Services (SSARS) 1 went into effect, launching a new era in financial reporting for nonpublic companies. SSARS 1, *Compilation and Review of Financial Statements*, was issued in December 1978 by the Accounting and Review Services Committee of the American Institute of Certified Public Accountants (AICPA). It paved the way for compilation and review, two new levels of nonaudit reports for nonpublic companies and, thus, replaced the unaudited disclaimer.

Much has been written about the nature of these new accounting services, and many people have speculated about the relative roles of compilation, review, and audit.

The purpose of this study is to assess the experiences, reactions, and attitudes of CPAs and bankers concerning compilation and review services. Study participants included 213 CPAs and 138 bankers. Their responses provide insight into the probable impact of SSARS 1 on the practice of accounting for nonpublic companies.

Before discussing our research methodology or study results, we shall review the background of SSARS 1 and shall introduce our research questions.

Evolution of SSARS 1

The formal rules pertaining to unaudited financial statements date back to 1949, when Statement on Auditing Procedure (SAP) 23 was issued.

This statement required that a warning, such as "Prepared From Books Without Audit," appear predominantly on each page of unaudited financial statements that are presented on the accountant's stationery without further comment. A disclaimer of opinion was not required on these unaudited statements. SAP 23 applied only to unaudited statements presented on the accountant's stationery, not to plain-paper reports. If plain paper was used, the accountant was not required to use any warning statements; however, the committee on auditing procedure discouraged the use of plain-paper statements.

SAP 23 became part of the *Codification of Statements on Auditing Procedure* that was issued by the AICPA in 1951. These requirements for unaudited statements remained in effect until 1963, when the Institute published Statement on Auditing Procedure 33, which consolidated and replaced previous pronouncements of the committee on auditing procedure. In relation to unaudited statements, this pronouncement stated the following:

> When no audit has been performed, or the auditing procedures performed are insignificant in the circumstances, any financial statements with which the independent auditor is in any way associated should be clearly and conspicuously marked on each page as unaudited, whether accompanied by his comments or not. It is preferable that a disclaimer of opinion accompany all such statements; when they are accompanied by comments the independent auditor must issue a disclaimer of opinion. Such a disclaimer of opinion may read as follows:
>
> > The accompanying balance sheet as of November 30, 19___ and the related statements of income and retained earnings for the year then ended were not audited by us and we express no opinion on them.

The committee on auditing procedure continued to consider the issues related to unaudited financial statements. In 1967, after considerable work, the committee issued SAP 38, *Unaudited Financial Statements*. This statement subsequently became codified as section 516 of the AICPA Statement on Auditing Standards (SAS) 1, *Codification of Auditing Standards and Procedures* (1972). It specified the rules governing unaudited statements for nonpublic companies prior to the issuance of SSARS 1.[1] Paragraph 516.04 of SAS 1 states

> A disclaimer of opinion should accompany unaudited financial statements with which the certified public accountant is associated. The disclaimer of opinion is the means by which the certified public accountant clearly indicates the fact that he has not audited the financial statements and accordingly does not express an opinion on them. An example of such a disclaimer of opinion is as follows:

---

1. Section 516 of SAS 1 was superseded by SAS 26, *Association With Financial Statements*, in November 1979. SAS 26 governs unaudited financial statements of public companies.

The accompanying balance sheet of X Company as of December 31, 19___, and the related statements of income and retained earnings and changes in financial position for the year then ended were not audited by us and accordingly we do not express an opinion on them.

(Signature and date)

The disclaimer of opinion may accompany the unaudited financial statements, or it may be placed directly on them. In addition, each page of the financial statements should be clearly and conspicuously marked as unaudited.

Thus, prior to the adoption of SSARS 1, a disclaimer was required to accompany all unaudited financial statements with which a CPA was associated.

As Alan Winters noted, "The nature and extent of procedures to be performed in unaudited statement engagements and the disclosure requirements for general-use and internal-use unaudited statements have posed the most difficult problems."[2] In his study, Winters found that CPA firms varied both in their review procedures and in their disclosures.

In response to such problems, the AICPA issued the *Guide for Engagements of CPAs to Prepare Unaudited Financial Statements* in 1975.[3] This extensive document served as the basis for preparation of unaudited financial statements until July 1979, when SSARS 1 took effect.

The cover letter to the exposure draft of SSARS 1 stated

With respect to entities whose securities are not publicly traded, existing AICPA pronouncements do not meet the needs of such entities for different levels of accounting and review services, the needs of users of the financial statements of those entities for different forms of assurance, or the needs of CPAs who prepare or review those statements for specific guidance. . . .

This view was shared by members of the accounting profession and users of financial statements.

In its 1976 report, the AICPA Committee on Generally Accepted Accounting Principles for Smaller and/or Closely Held Businesses stated

The committee . . . believes that a more informative CPA's report, one which refers to the accounting services rendered and distinguishes them from auditing procedures, should be considered. Finally, the "internal use only" disclaimer should be reevaluated and consideration should be given to allowing the CPA to be associated with financial statements where some or all footnote disclosures have been omitted if the CPA's report includes an appropriate notice to the reader about such omissions without necessarily identifying them in detail.[4]

---

2. Alan J. Winters, "Unaudited Statements: Review Procedures and Disclosures," *Journal of Accountancy* 142 (July 1976): 52.
3. AICPA, Task Force on Unaudited Financial Statements, *Guide for Engagements of CPAs to Prepare Unaudited Financial Statements* (New York: AICPA, 1975).
4. AICPA, *Report of the Committee on Generally Accepted Accounting Principles for Smaller and/or Closely Held Businesses* (New York: AICPA, 1976), p. 18.

In addition, the Commission on Auditors' Responsibilities (Cohen commission) observed

> The view that users will misunderstand different levels of assurance underestimates users' capabilities. According to this view, any time the auditor is associated with information, users will assume it has been audited. This conclusion is predetermined by present reporting requirements. If the only form of assurance given is an opinion on financial statements, then users have no opportunity to understand other types of assurance. . . . The only way users will become informed is for auditors to change the traditional approach to reporting.[5]

Winters, in a study he conducted on banker perceptions of unaudited financial statements, found the following:

> Loan officer beliefs concerning unaudited statement reviews suggest yet another conflict between the profession's posture regarding unaudited statements and bankers' attitudes toward CPA responsibility. Professional standards specifically state that the accountant has no duty to apply any auditing procedures. Nowhere do these standards state that a review of any type is required for unaudited statements. However, one-third of the bankers believe the CPA should perform some audit procedures, and the majority of loan officers believes CPAs should at least take some positive review steps such as inquiry.[6]

This finding further underscored the need for reevaluation of unaudited services performed by CPAs.

In response to such concerns, in 1975 the AICPA established the accounting and review services (ARS) subcommittee of the auditing standards executive committee (presently the Auditing Standards Board). In 1977 the committee was elevated to its current status as a senior technical committee of the AICPA, with the attendant rights and responsibilities to issue separate pronouncements and establish standards.

The result of the committee's work to date, in addition to SSARS 1, has been the issuance of SSARS 2, *Reporting on Comparative Financial Statements* (1979); an exposure draft on prescribed forms; and an exposure draft on communications with predecessor accountants. Clearly, the most important result has been the introduction of compilation and review services.

---

5. AICPA, *Report, Conclusions, and Recommendations of the Commission on Auditors' Responsibilities* (New York: AICPA, 1978), pp. 66–67.
6. Winters, "Banker Perceptions of Unaudited Financial Statements," *CPA Journal* 45 (August 1975): 32.

Compilation and Review

The accounting and review services committee extensively considered the views of CPAs and users in formulating SSARS 1. Thomas P. Kelley, then the AICPA's managing director of technical services, noted

> The changes in practice proposed in the exposure draft were revolutionary. And like all revolutionary proposals, they sparked controversy. Almost 400 letters of comment—an unprecedented response—were received during the seven-month exposure period. In addition, 2,100 members returned completed questionnaires to the AICPA in conjunction with their participation in member forums sponsored by forty-four state societies.[7]

Earle V. King, who was a member of the committee, and Joseph T. Cote reported, "Due to this response, the committee amended and revised the exposure draft extensively."[8]

The resulting pronouncement allows an accountant who submits financial statements that he has not audited to issue either a compilation or a review report. The pronouncement considers the nature of procedures to be performed for each service and the format of the underlying accountant's report.

Figure 1.1 describes the various forms of reporting services now available and includes a sample accountant's report for each.

A Compilation Engagement

Much like the unaudited disclaimer issued under section 516 of SAS 1, the compilation report overtly states that the accountant expresses no opinion on the financial statements. Unlike the disclaimer, however, the compilation report must state that the accountant compiled the financial statements and that they are representations of management. Further, the ARS committee has eliminated the concept of internal-use-only financial statements with which the CPA could formerly be associated.

SSARS 1 provides the following specific compilation standards:

10. The accountant should possess a level of knowledge of the accounting principles and practices of the industry in which the entity operates that

---

7. Thomas P. Kelley, "Compilation and Review—A Revolution in Practice," *CPA Journal* 49 (April 1979): 19.
8. Earle V. King and Joseph T. Cote, "Compilation and Review," *California CPA Quarterly* 47 (June 1979): 9.

Figure 1.1
Comparison of Audit, Review, and Compilation Services

	Audit	Review	Compilation
Description	An audit involves the critical evaluation of a company's financial statements to form the basis for expressing an opinion on the financial statements taken as a whole. Evidence is gathered through inspection of underlying accounting records and a study and evaluation of internal accounting controls. Observations (e.g., of the inventory taking) and inquiries are made and analytical review procedures are carried out. Confirmations and representations also are obtained. The extent of those procedures depends on the accountant's evaluation of existing facts and circumstances.	A review encompasses performance of inquiry and analytical procedures to provide the accountant with a reasonable basis for expressing limited assurance that there are no material changes that should be made to the financial statements for them to be in conformity with generally accepted accounting principles.	The compilation service consists of presenting information supplied by management in financial statement format. The compilation does not involve an undertaking to express any assurance on those statements.
What Assurance Can the Accountant Give?	Positive assurance [Generally accepted auditing standards require the accountant to perform procedures necessary to determine if the financial	Limited—Although the review may bring significant matters affecting your financial statements to the accountant's attention, it does not provide as-	None—In a compilation, there is no examination or review of financial statements. Quite literally, the accountant compiles information supplied by man-

statements are presented fairly in conformity with generally accepted accounting principles, consistently applied. The unqualified audit report states that in the accountant's opinion, based upon this examination, the financial statements are presented fairly.]

What Can the Accountant Report?

Financial statements which are audited are accompanied by a report:

- Stating that an examination was made in accordance with generally accepted auditing standards;
- Indicating that the examination included all auditing procedures considered necessary in the circumstances and, ordinarily;
- Expressing an opinion whether the financial statements (in all material respects) are presented in accordance with consistently applied generally accepted accounting principles.

surance that he will become aware of all significant matters that would be disclosed in an audit.

Financial statements which are reviewed are accompanied by a report stating that:

- A review was performed in accordance with standards established by the AICPA;
- All information included in the statements is the representation of management (owners);
- A review consists principally of inquiries of company personnel and analytical procedures applied to financial data;
- A review is substantially less in scope than an audit, and that no opinion is expressed, and;

agement into a format appropriate to the company's industry.

Financial statements which are compiled without audit or review are accompanied by a report stating that:

- A compilation has been performed;
- A compilation is limited to presenting in the form of financial statements information that is the representation of management (owners); and
- The statements have not been audited or reviewed and, accordingly, no opinion or any other form of assurance is expressed on them.

7

Figure 1.1

Comparison of Audit, Review, and Compilation Services (*continued*)

	Audit	Review	Compilation
What Can the Accountant Report? (*continued*)		• The accountant is not aware of any material modifications that should be made to the statements for them to be in conformity with generally accepted accounting principles (other than those modifications, if any, indicated in the report).	
Sample Report	We have examined the balance sheet of *ABC Company* as of December 31, 19XX, and the related statements of income, retained earnings and changes in financial position for the year then ended. Our examination was made in accordance with generally accepted auditing standards and, accordingly, included tests of the accounting records and such other auditing procedures as	We have reviewed the accompanying balance sheet of *ABC Company* as of December 31, 19XX, and the related statements of income, retained earnings and changes in financial position for the year then ended, in accordance with standards established by the AICPA. All information included in these financial statements is the representation of the management (owners) of *ABC Company*.	The accompanying balance sheet of *ABC Company* as of December 31, 19XX, and the related statements of income, retained earnings and changes in financial position for the year then ended have been compiled by us. A compilation is limited to presenting in the form of financial statements information that is the representation of management (owners). We have not

we considered necessary in the circumstances.

In our opinion, such financial statements present fairly the financial position of *ABC Company* at December 31, 19XX, and the results of its operations and the changes in its financial position for the year then ended, in conformity with generally accepted accounting principles applied on a bas's consistent with that of the preceding year.

A review consists principally of inquiries and analytical procedures applied to financial data. It is substantially less in scope than an examination in accordance with generally accepted auditing standards, the objective of which is the expression of an opinion regarding the financial statements taken as a whole.

Based on our review, we are not aware of any material modifications that should be made to the accompanying financial statements in order for them to be in conformity with generally accepted accounting principles.

audited or reviewed the accompanying financial statements and, accordingly, do not express an opinion or any other form of assurance on them.*

*In the absence of all disclosures, a third paragraph must be included, indicating that such disclosures might have influenced users. *Compilation with disclosures* and *compilation without disclosures* are used throughout this monograph as abbreviated references for *compilation of financial statements with adequate disclosure* and *compilation of financial statements without adequate disclosure*, respectively.

Source: Adapted from Kenneth J. Dirkes and John R. Deming, "Audit, Compilation or Review?" *CPA Journal* 50 (April 1980): 86–87.

will enable him to compile financial statements that are appropriate in form for an entity operating in that industry. . . .

11. The accountant should possess a general understanding of the nature of the entity's business transactions, the form of its accounting records, the stated qualifications of its accounting personnel, the accounting basis on which the financial statements are to be presented, and the form and content of the financial statements. . . .

12. The accountant is not required to make inquiries or perform other procedures to verify, corroborate, or review information supplied by the entity. . . .

13. Before issuing his report, the accountant should read the compiled financial statements and consider whether such financial statements appear to be appropriate in form and free from obvious material errors. . . .

14. Financial statements compiled without audit or review by an accountant should be accompanied by a report stating that
    a. A compilation has been performed.
    b. A compilation is limited to representing in the form of financial statements information that is the representation of management (owners).
    c. The financial statements have not been audited or reviewed and, accordingly, the accountant does not express an opinion or any other form of assurance on them. . . .

15. The date of completion of the compilation should be used as the date of the accountant's report.

16. Each page of the financial statements compiled by the accountant should include a reference such as "See Accountant's Compilation Report."[9]

Notwithstanding the efforts of the ARS committee, compilations have not been universally accepted by practitioners. One leading standard-setter noted

> I do not believe that the preparation of compiled financial statements within the framework of [SSARS] 1 is a professional service. While the objectives of our professional pronouncements should include a recognition of clients' needs, our purpose should be to meet such needs without diluting our standards.[10]

A Review Engagement

The ARS committee's sanctioning of the review report provides the greatest departure from the pre-SSARS era. The review introduces a middle-level report in which the CPA overtly provides limited assurance

---

9. AICPA, Statement on Standards for Accounting and Review Services 1, *Compilation and Review of Financial Statements* (New York: AICPA, 1978), paragraphs 10–16.
10. Charles Chazen, "Compilation of Financial Statements—A Professional Service," *Journal of Accountancy* 146 (September 1978): 99.

that the accompanying financial statements are in conformity with generally accepted accounting principles. Thus, under SSARS 1, the CPA is no longer limited to either a disclaimer of opinion on financial statements for nonpublic companies or expression of an unqualified opinion in conjunction with an audit. A substantial portion of this monograph is concerned with the impact of the review on the practice of accounting for nonpublic companies.

The specific review standards under SSARS 1 include the following:

24. The accountant should possess a level of knowledge of the accounting principles and practices of the industry in which the entity operates and an understanding of the entity's business that will provide him, through the performance of inquiry and analytical procedures, with a reasonable basis for expressing limited assurance that there are no material modifications that should be made to the financial statements in order for the statements to be in conformity with generally accepted accounting principles. . . .

26. The accountant's understanding of the entity's business should include a general understanding of the entity's organization, its operating characteristics, and the nature of its assets, liabilities, revenues, and expenses. . . .

27. The accountant's inquiry and analytical procedures should ordinarily consist of the following:
    a. Inquiries concerning the entity's accounting principles and practices and the methods followed in applying them.
    b. Inquiries concerning the entity's procedures for recording, classifying, and summarizing transactions, and accumulating information for disclosure in the financial statements.
    c. Analytical procedures designed to identify relationships and individual items that appear to be unusual. For the purposes of this statement, analytical procedures consist of (1) comparison of the financial statements with statements for comparable prior period(s), (2) comparison of the financial statements with anticipated results, if available (for example, budgets and forecasts), and (3) study of the relationships of the elements of the financial statements that would be expected to conform to a predictable pattern based on the entity's experience. In applying these procedures, the accountant should consider the types of matters that required accounting adjustments in preceding periods. Examples of relationships of elements in financial statements that would be expected to conform to a predictable pattern may be the relationships between changes in sales and changes in accounts receivable and expense accounts that ordinarily fluctuate with sales, and between changes in property, plant, and equipment and changes in depreciation expense and other accounts that may be affected, such as maintenance and repairs.
    d. Inquiries concerning actions taken at meetings of stockholders, board of directors, committees of the board of directors, or comparable meetings that may affect the financial statements.
    e. Reading the financial statements to consider, on the basis of information coming to the accountant's attention, whether the financial statements appear to conform with generally accepted accounting principles.

    f.   Obtaining reports from other accountants, if any, who have been engaged to audit or review the financial statements of significant components of the reporting entity, its subsidiaries, and other investees.

    g.   Inquiries of persons having responsibility for financial and accounting matters concerning (1) whether the financial statements have been prepared in conformity with generally accepted accounting principles consistently applied, (2) changes in the entity's business activities or accounting principles and practices, (3) matters as to which questions have arisen in the course of applying the foregoing procedures, and (4) events subsequent to the date of the financial statements that would have a material effect on the financial statements.

28. Knowledge acquired in the performance of audits of the entity's financial statements, compilation of the financial statements, or other accounting services may result in modification of the review procedures described in the preceding paragraph. However, such modification would not reduce the degree of responsibility the accountant assumes with respect to the financial statements he has reviewed.

29. A review does not contemplate a study and evaluation of internal accounting control, tests of accounting records and of responses to inquiries by obtaining corroborating evidential matter, and certain other procedures ordinarily performed during an audit. Thus, a review does not provide assurance that the accountant will become aware of all significant matters that would be disclosed in an audit. . . .

32. Financial statements reviewed by an accountant should be accompanied by a report stating that—

    a.   A review was performed in accordance with standards established by the American Institute of Certified Public Accountants.

    b.   All information included in the financial statements is the representation of the management (owners) of the entity.

    c.   A review consists principally of inquiries of company personnel and analytical procedures applied to financial data.

    d.   A review is substantially less in scope than an audit, the objective of which is the expression of an opinion regarding the financial statements taken as a whole and, accordingly, no such opinion is expressed.

    e.   The accountant is not aware of any material modifications that should be made to the financial statements in order for them to be in conformity with generally accepted accounting principles, other than those modifications, if any, indicated in his report.

Any other procedures that the accountant might have performed before or during the review engagement, including those performed in connection with a compilation of the financial statements, should not be described in his report.

33. The date of completion of the accountant's inquiry and analytical procedures should be used as the date of his report.

34. Each page of the financial statements reviewed by the accountant should include a reference such as "See Accountant's Review Report."[11]

---

11. AICPA, SSARS 1, paragraphs 24–34.

As in the case of compilations, the concept of the review has generated some criticism. One practitioner, Harry Brown, observes, "Limited assurance is a term that could cause problems of interpretation. When or how does the practitioner determine that this point of comfort has been reached?"[12] In reference to SSARS 1 in general, Brown notes the following:

> As a partner in a modest-sized firm, the author has been delighted when some users understand the differences between audited and unaudited statements. To enlighten such users on the material in the SSARS may not be feasible. To outsiders, CPAs either performed an audit and rendered an opinion—or they did not and gave a disclaimer. Other presentations will confuse, and may expose CPAs to unnecessary liability.[13]

Generally, practitioners and bankers are responding favorably to SSARS 1, although some bankers are in fact confused about the differences between the various forms of unaudited reports currently and formerly available.

Finally, it should be noted that SSARS 1 made no changes to audits of nonpublic companies; therefore, this chapter ignores that facet of figure 1.1.

Research Questions

Many people have speculated about the impact of SSARS 1 on the practice of accounting for nonpublic companies. Much of this speculation has centered on the nature of any shift from formerly available to currently available services, the factors that might influence such a shift, the relative costs of the services, and the overall reactions and attitudes of CPAs and users. This study was undertaken to provide insight into these and related issues.

The specific study issues and subissues are the following:

1. What are the actual and the projected shifts from audits to reviews or compilations?

   a. What are CPAs' and bankers' estimates of the actual movement by companies from audit to review or compilation services?

   b. What are CPAs' and bankers' estimates of the probable shift within the next year from audit to review or compilation services?

2. What are the actual and the projected shifts from previous unaudited services to compilations, reviews, or audits?

   a. What are CPAs' and bankers' estimates of the actual movement

---

12. Harry G. Brown, "Compilation and Review—A Step Forward?" *CPA Journal* 49 (May 1979): 21.
13. *Ibid.*, p. 23.

by companies from previous unaudited statements to compilations, reviews, or audits?

    b. What are CPAs' and bankers' estimates of the probable composition of services in one year for those companies that provided unaudited financial statements prior to SSARS 1?

3. What factors influence the selection of services?

4. What are the relative costs of compilations, reviews, and audits?

5. What are lenders' perceptions of appropriate conditions for compilations, reviews, and audits?

6. What are the overall attitudes of CPAs and bankers toward compilations, reviews, and audits and the role of the various services in personal financial statements?

In May and June of 1980, a broadly based national sample of CPAs and bankers completed questionnaires constructed around these issues. Chapter 2 discusses the methodology used in constructing the questionnaires and selecting population samples, and chapters 3, 4, and 5 analyze the responses of the bankers and CPAs. The responses should assist the accounting profession in developing the market for compilation and review services.

Many people had speculated that the adoption of SSARS 1 would lead to a dramatic movement away from audits and toward reviews or compilations. On this subject, the *Wall Street Journal* noted, "Scores of small businesses are planning to eliminate audits and substitute a far less expensive procedure known as 'review.'"[14] We asked CPAs and bankers to estimate the amount of shift away from audits since the adoption of SSARS 1 and to project any additional shift within the next year.

A primary reason for the adoption of SSARS 1 was that the ARS committee members "were convinced that there are different levels of services being performed by CPAs and, therefore, there should be different levels of reporting."[15] A previously unanswered question addressed by this study is how nonpublic companies would avail themselves of the new services. Thus, the second research issue relates to the movement away from the previous unaudited services to compilation, review, or audit services.

The first two issues concern the aggregate movement between the various services by nonpublic companies; in individual situations, the reasons for such shifts are relevant to preparers and users of financial

---

14. *Wall Street Journal,* 14 May 1979.
15. King and Cote, "Compilation and Review," p. 9.

statements. To isolate these factors, the CPAs and bankers were presented with several cases and asked to rank the relative significance of a given list of factors.

One of the most widely discussed issues since the adoption of SSARS 1 has been the relative costs of the services that are now available. The *Wall Street Journal,* among others, has considered this issue in estimating the impact of compilation and review. Until now, however, no actual data seem to have been gathered on the subject. This study, at least in part, fills this void. The CPAs in the study were asked to estimate the number of hours required to complete a review or compilation engagement in relation to the number of hours needed to complete an audit.

To provide the bankers with an unconstrained avenue for commenting on the roles of the various services, we asked them, in a series of open-ended questions, to indicate the conditions under which each service is most appropriate.

CPAs and bankers also were asked a series of questions concerning their overall attitudes and reactions to the services now available. These questions were general in nature in order to provide an overall profile of the likely impact of SSARS 1 on the practice of accounting for nonpublic companies.

2

Research Methodology

This chapter describes the methodology applied to investigate the experiences and attitudes of CPAs and bankers concerning compilations, reviews, and audits. Diverse samples of professionals from both groups completed questionnaires that addressed these issues. This chapter discusses the sampling plan, response data, and questionnaire construction.

Sampling Plan

The study was designed to be national in scope. CPAs and bankers were selected from New York City and Paterson in the Northeast, Atlanta and Charlotte in the Southeast, Kansas City and Topeka/Lawrence in the Midwest, and Los Angeles and Fresno in the Far West.

In devising the sampling plan, we recognized that significant differences in attitudes and responses can exist in cities of different sizes and regions. Disaggregated information should prove useful to the accounting profession in its study of the markets for compilation and review services.

CPA Selection

The accounting profession is structured in the form of a pyramid, tapering from a large base of local firms to relatively few national firms. In order to assess potential firm-size effects, the sample included both national and local firms. Specifically, seven of the largest fifteen national firms participated in the study, as well as thirty-eight local firms. In order to reflect the diversity of local practice units, the local-firm category included firms with one office or with several offices within one region.

To encourage the participation of individuals from the seven national firms, we met with an executive from the national office of each firm and secured a commitment that the firm would participate, conditioned upon a guarantee that the firm's name would not be disclosed in the results. Subsequently, all questionnaires for the firm were mailed to the executive with whom we had met. He then attached a letter encouraging participation and forwarded the questionnaires to individuals in the firm's practice offices. One questionnaire was sent to an office executive in each participating office; up to six other questionnaires, identical except for the omission of any questions concerning overall client mix, were distributed to line partners and staff in each of these offices. (The two questionnaires are presented in Appendixes A and B.) Upon completion, the respondents mailed the questionnaires directly to us.

Although not all seven firms had an office in each sample city, responses were received from individuals from at least one national firm in each location.

The participation of local firms was secured in a different manner. We telephoned a senior partner in each multioffice firm and asked for a commitment that his firm would participate. The executive distributed questionnaires to each practice office included in the sample and requested their participation. An executive partner in each practice office was asked to complete the questionnaire in Appendix A, and up to five line partners and staff completed the Appendix B questionnaire.

Single-office local firms were also solicited by telephone. Ten firms from each of the large cities (New York, Los Angeles, Atlanta, and Kansas City) and five from the smaller cities agreed to participate. One partner in each firm was asked to complete the Appendix A questionnaire. Discussions with these participants indicated that it would have been inappropriate to request the involvement of more than one person from each firm.

Banker Selection

In an approach similar to the one used to involve national CPA firms, we met with an executive (typically at least a senior vice president) from each selected bank to secure the bank's participation. In all, thirty banks agreed to participate.

Bank operations are largely regulated by diverse federal and state statutes. For example, some states allow branch banking while others require unit operations. In unit states, bank holding companies have developed in order to achieve economies of scale.

As a result, there is no clear definition of a "large bank." Therefore, we decided not to stratify banks on the basis of size and not to isolate a bank-size effect in the results. Nonetheless, we have analyzed selected information from a general large/small bank perspective.

The questionnaires to be completed by the loan officers (reproduced in Appendix C) were mailed to the participating executive in each bank for distribution through intrabank channels. The bank executive attached a cover letter indicating the bank's participation in this study. Again, all questionnaires were returned directly to us.

Response Data

Overall data about the distribution of questionnaires to CPAs and the responses received from them are presented in figure 2.1.

Figure 2.1
Overall CPA Distribution and Responses

	Number Distributed to Practice Office	Number Returned	Response Rate
National Firms			
Questionnaire for office executives	41	22	54%
Questionnaire for line individuals	216	138	64%
National firm total	257	160	62%
Local Firms			
Questionnaire for office executives	65	39	60%
Questionnaire for line individuals	25	14	56%
Local firm total	90	53	59%
Total	347	213	61%

Note: To ensure anonymity of participating firms, responses by city are not presented.

Although 213 questionnaires were returned by the CPAs, not all respondents answered all questions. Also, review of the completed questionnaires resulted in the deletion of unusable or unreasonable responses to some questions. For these reasons, usable responses on individual questions vary and are identified in the analysis.

Review of the background data from the questionnaires suggests that the respondents are highly educated (more than 97 percent have at least four years of college), with an average of over fifteen years in public accounting. Furthermore, they indicate a strong familiarity with the SSARS pronouncements.

Figure 2.2 shows the distribution of questionnaires to the bankers, and their responses, by city.

Figure 2.2
Bank Distribution and Responses

City	Number of Banks	Number of Questionnaires Distributed	Number Returned	Response Rate
New York	4	51	25	49%
Paterson	4	24	14	58%
Los Angeles	4	45	20	44%
Fresno	4	10	9	90%
Atlanta	4	35	29	83%
Charlotte	3	34	16	47%
Kansas City	3	19	15	79%
Topeka/Lawrence	4	18	10	56%
Total	30	236	138	58%

Note: For reasons discussed in reference to the CPA data, usable responses vary across specific questions.

Review of the background data indicates that the respondents are highly educated. (More than 90 percent have at least four years of college.) They average more than ten years' experience as a loan officer, and a majority process more than fifty loans per year.

In both the CPA and the bank surveys, we decided to sample on a prior-contact rather than a blind random basis. This decision was based primarily on response-rate considerations. Over 61 percent of the CPAs and 58 percent of the bankers contacted responded to the questionnaires. Previous studies suggest that such high response rates are likely to result from the prior-contact approach. On the other hand, it is generally known that studies conducted on a blind random basis typically result in a very low response rate (say, 20 percent). Therefore, we decided to compromise some randomness in return for a substantially higher response rate.

In any survey research, the question arises of how to evaluate nonrespondents. Because of the high response rates, nonresponse bias is not a significant problem in this study. Moreover, the prior-contact approach applied in this study is not amenable to follow-up procedures, since that would have meant asking CPA and bank executives to distribute second requests to those not responding. Such a procedure would have raised questions among both the executives and the participants about the actual anonymity of the results. In light of the high response rates, it was decided not to pursue this approach.

An early/late response surrogate was inappropriate, since substantially all responses were received within a two-week period.

Questionnaire Construction

Before this study, little national data existed on the impact of the SSARS pronouncements on CPAs and bankers. The purpose of this study is to generate an original data base on these subjects. Therefore, the study is exploratory in nature. Research literature supports the use of the questionnaire technique in this situation because it is well suited to the eliciting of attitudes and experimental data from a diverse group of participants.

The questionnaires were designed to address the study issues identified in chapter 1:

1. The shift from audits to reviews or compilations.

2. The shift from previous unaudited services to compilations, reviews, or audits.

3. Factors influencing the selection of services.

4. The relative costs of compilations, reviews, and audits.

5. Lenders' perceptions of appropriate conditions for compilations, reviews, and audits.

6. Overall attitudes of CPAs and bankers toward compilations, reviews, and audits and the role of the various services in personal financial statements.

To research movements between the various services, the questionnaires included two general types of inquiries. One series relates to actual shifts since SSARS 1 became effective in 1979; the other focuses on projected shifts. Respondents completed the questionnaires during May and June of 1980; therefore, actual experience covers the first year under SSARS 1. The projection questions ask respondents to predict any shifts within one year from completion of the questionnaire.

We used standard analysis of variance (ANOVA) and t-tests to statistically evaluate any differences between various subgroup classifications (such as regional differences). Because of the nature of the sampling plan, the responses generally fall into relatively large but unequal cell sizes, with unequal variances. As is generally known, the t- and F-tests are robust with respect to moderate departures from the hypothesis of homogeneity of variance. Nonetheless, in order to mitigate the possible effects of differences in variances, the appropriate t-test (using separate rather than pooled variances) was used when variance differences existed. No such adjustment is possible for the F-test. In any event, the power of the significance tests is uncertain as a result of differences in variances across samples.

To identify factors that influence the selection of services, we presented participants with three hypothetical client situations and asked them to rank a list of factors according to relative influence on the selection of a service. The specific factors presented to CPAs were largely the same as the ones presented to bankers. To mitigate order effects, the placement of factors was randomly varied for each of the three situations in each context. These rankings were evaluated through use of the nonparametric Kendall's coefficient of concordance test (W).

The actual costs of auditing and accounting services are, of course, proprietary in nature. Any attempt to solicit this information would clearly have resulted in a low response rate. Therefore, it was necessary to use a surrogate measure. In order to determine the most realistic cost substitute, discussions were held with executives from various CPA firms. Their overall conclusion was that relative hours translate meaningfully into relative costs. Thus, questions were posed in terms of the relative hours required to perform the various services. All CPAs participating in the study were asked to compare relative hours in different situations relating to continuing and prospective clients.

Again, subgroup comparisons were based upon ANOVA and t-tests.

Participating loan officers were presented with a series of open-ended questions relating to the appropriate conditions for each of the available services. The results of these questions are presented in chapter 4.

We used a Likert-type scale to assess the overall attitudes of CPAs and lenders toward the various services. The data were treated as interval, and the appropriate parametric ANOVA and t-tests were used in analyzing the results on a subgroup basis.

Again, the reader is referred to Appendixes A, B, and C for a presentation of the questionnaires.

Experimental Realism

Several steps were taken to ensure the experimental realism of the research instruments. Bank executives and CPA partners participated in the original design of the questionnaires. The factors included in the ranking questions as well as the use of hours as a surrogate for cost resulted from these discussions. Prior to pretesting, drafts of the questionnaires were distributed to selected bank and CPA executives. After their suggestions were incorporated, the questionnaires were pretested at a bank and at national and local CPA firms in a location not included in the final study. The final questionnaires included appropriate revisions.

Comments from the 351 participants indicate that the questionnaires meaningfully addressed the issues under investigation. Furthermore, the responses to the open-ended questions and the average completion time of approximately thirty minutes indicate that respondents completed the questionnaires thoughtfully.

Study Limitations

To generate a high response rate, we decided to sample on a prior-contact basis. As a result, the participants were not selected randomly. Therefore, the ability to generalize the results is somewhat limited.

Although bankers and CPAs were selected from the same cities, it was not possible to sample from the same population of companies. Thus, the results do not completely overlap.

Finally, although CPA and bank executives assisted in the design of the research instruments, problems of interpretation resulted in some unusable responses. This problem is inevitable in any questionnaire research.

3

Study Results—CPAs

According to key leaders of the accounting profession, the introduction of compilation and review services represents a dramatic change in reporting for nonpublic companies. The first chairman of the accounting and review services committee, William R. Gregory, observed

> The very suggestion that a CPA express assurance in connection with financial statements that have not been audited is heresy to many members of the profession. Others hold that the realities of the business world and the increasing complexity of professional standards have created a need for a new line of assurance which is less than that expressed as a result of an audit made in accordance with generally accepted auditing standards but certainly greater than that included in the present disclaimer on unaudited financial statements. It is my opinion that the profession should step up to its responsibility to those it serves in other than audit engagements and accept the notion that the use of such financial statements by third parties creates a justified expectation for some form of assurance. The profession can and should accept that responsibility; it is an idea whose time has arrived.[1]

The purpose of this chapter is to report and analyze the responses of the CPAs participating in this study in terms of the six research issues discussed in chapter 1. The responses are presented in the aggregate and by firm size, city size, and region.

---

1. William R. Gregory, "Unaudited but OK?" *Journal of Accountancy* 145 (February 1978): 61.

The Shift From Audits to Reviews or Compilations

One of the most profound issues addressed by this study is the nature of the shift from audits to lesser forms of service. Indeed, users of financial statements have expressed concern that such a shift might become widespread.[2] This section reports on CPAs' estimates of actual and projected movements.

The office executives from the national and multioffice local firms and the participating individuals from the single-office firms responded to questions about the actual movement to a lower level of service. On the average, the sixty-one respondents estimated that 2.5 percent of their previous nonpublic audit clients switched to a review and 0.1 percent switched to a compilation with disclosures. These aggregate figures are broken down by firm size, city size, and region in figures 3.1, 3.2, and 3.3 respectively. The measure of statistical significance is based on the t-statistic for figures 3.1 and 3.2 and the F-statistic for figure 3.3.

In interpreting the tables, the reader must consider two points: The statistical comparisons are vertical, and the probability measure (p) refers to the level of statistical significance. For example, in figure 3.1 the movement to review experienced by national firms (2.4 percent) is compared with that of local firms (2.6 percent). Further, the p of .83 means that, given no difference in the means across the two populations, there is an 83 percent probability that these results could happen by chance. The lower this probability, the greater the likelihood that the sample differences reflect actual differences in the populations. In this study, differences are considered statistically significant at a probability (p) of .05 or less.

In the aggregate and throughout all categories, CPAs perceived only slight movement away from audits to reviews or compilations. There are no statistically significant differences based on firm size, city size, or region. These results are consistent with the predictions of CPAs sampled by Brasseaux and Pearl, who note, "Most firms expect the demand for services to remain the same and do not expect a 'scale down' in engagements from audit to review or compilation."[3]

The CPAs were also requested to project any movement away from audits within the next year. The sixty-one CPAs responding to these questions predicted a shift to review of an additional 2.1 percent and to compilation with disclosures of 0.3 percent within the next year. No further breakdowns are presented since at $\alpha = .05$ there are no significant differences across firm size, city size, or region.

---

2. James R. Waterston, "Compilation, Review and the Division for CPA Firms: A Banker's Perspective," *Journal of Commercial Bank Lending* (August 1979): 11–18.
3. J. H. Brasseaux and Daniel Pearl, "Reviews and Compilation: An Analysis and Survey of Their Expected Impact," *Louisiana Certified Public Accountant* (Winter/Spring 1979/80): 38.

Figure 3.1
CPA Questionnaire
Movement From Audits to Reviews or Compilations
Disclosure by Firm Size

	Responses	To Review	To Compilation With Disclosure
National firms	22	2.4%	0%
Local firms	39	2.6%	0.2%
Probability (p)		.83	.33

Figure 3.2
CPA Questionnaire
Movement From Audits to Reviews or Compilations
Disclosure by City Size

	Responses	To Review	To Compilation With Disclosure
Large cities	42	3.0%	0.1%
Small cities	19	1.5%	0.1%
Probability (p)		.15	.93

Figure 3.3
CPA Questionnaire
Movement From Audits to Reviews or Compilations
Disclosure by Region

	Responses	To Review	To Compilation With Disclosure
Northeast	12	2.4%	0%
Southeast	18	2.3%	0%
Midwest	14	3.6%	0.5%
Far West	17	1.9%	0%
Probability (p)		.80	.12

Given the results for actual and projected shift away from audits, it is clear that CPAs participating in this study perceived SSARS 1 to have had, and to be likely in the near future to have, a very slight impact on their existing audit clients.

As discussed in the next chapter, banker responses present an interesting comparison. On the whole, bankers estimate a greater movement away from audits than do CPAs.

The Shift From Previous Unaudited Services to Compilations, Reviews, or Audits

The primary impetus for the SSARS pronouncements was the recognition by the accounting profession of the need to clarify the nature of "unaudited financial statements." Speaking for the ARS committee, William Gregory noted

> that such [unaudited] services should be defined and distinguished and that standards for their performance should be established. The committee, therefore, perceives three levels of service a CPA may perform with respect to financial statements: audit, review and compilation.[4]

The purpose of this analysis is to identify the impact of SSARS 1 on those clients formerly receiving unaudited services. More specifically, this section addresses the services provided to this group between the adoption of SSARS 1 and the completion of the questionnaires in May and June of 1980 and the projected services for the next year.

Current Distribution of Services

The office executives from the national and multioffice local firms and the respondents from the single-office firms were asked to estimate the current composition of services for their previously unaudited clients. On the average, the forty-five respondents indicated the following distribution: audits, 12.5 percent; reviews, 28.2 percent; and compilations, 59.3 percent.

It is interesting that the CPAs indicated that slightly over 40 percent of their clients who previously received no assurance were receiving a review or audit. In reference to this point, a local practitioner participating in this study observed

> Our firm is attempting to upgrade the previous unaudited financial statements to the review statements. This has the advantage of a better presentation as well as increasing our fees for the expanded services. We have been successful in this approach and hopefully will continue to be so. The client and the users of the financial statements are the major beneficiaries of the review statement but the accounting profession as a whole will benefit by producing a higher quality of work.

The overall results become even more interesting when disaggregated. Figures 3.4, 3.5, and 3.6 present the results by firm size, city size, and region respectively. The measure of statistical significance is based on the t-statistic for figures 3.4 and 3.5 and the F-statistic for figure 3.6. As indicated in figure 3.4, there is a firm-size effect regarding compilations; that is, there are statistically significant differences between the responses

---

4. Gregory, "Unaudited but OK?" pp. 63–64.

Figure 3.4
CPA Questionnaire
Shift From Unaudited Services to Compilation, Review, or Audit
Disclosure by Firm Size

	Responses	To Audit	To Review	To Compilation
National firms	12	23.3%	39.2%	37.5%
Local firms	33	8.6%	24.1%	67.3%
Probability (p)		.12	.12	.01*

*Differences are significant at α = .05.

Figure 3.5
CPA Questionnaire
Shift From Unaudited Services to Compilation, Review, or Audit
Disclosure by City Size

	Responses	To Audit	To Review	To Compilation
Large cities	30	12.3%	28.0%	59.7%
Small cities	15	13.0%	28.3%	58.7%
Probability (p)		.92	.97	.93

Figure 3.6
CPA Questionnaire
Shift From Unaudited Services to Compilation, Review, or Audit
Disclosure by Region

	Responses	To Audit	To Review	To Compilation
Northeast	7	10.0%	50.7%	39.3%
Southeast	12	19.5%	21.9%	58.6%
Midwest	12	9.2%	8.6%	82.2%
Far West	14	10.7%	39.1%	50.2%
Probability (p)		.60	.00*	.03*

*Differences are significant at α = .05.

of individuals from large firms and those of individuals from local firms. Clients of large firms tended to move to audits and reviews, while those of small firms opted for compilations.

Although it is difficult to pinpoint actual causes for these differences, there are reasonable explanations. Large firms tend to have larger clients, and the financial needs of these clients are more likely to suggest an upgrading of services than those of smaller companies. Also, local practice units have traditionally derived a significant portion of their revenue from nonaudit functions, while large firms have been more audit oriented.

An alternative explanation is that the level of service did not change substantially as a result of SSARS 1. Prior to SSARS 1, large firms may typically have been performing reviews and smaller firms compilations, while both were required to issue the same disclaimer of opinion. Under SSARS 1, they may only be reporting accurately on the level of service performed all along.

The original study design called for sampling by region in order to isolate any geographical effects. As is evident from figure 3.6, clients in the Midwest are far more likely to select a compilation, and less likely to select a review, than clients in the other regions. Although it is not possible to explain this with certainty, it seems that the agricultural nature of the region influences the emphasis on compilations. Discussions with individuals participating in the study support this conclusion.

Projected Distribution of Services

Respondents to the question on current composition of services for previously unaudited clients also addressed the likely composition in one year. Their overall predictions are presented in figure 3.7. For comparative purposes, their responses regarding current composition are also presented. Although it appears that the CPAs anticipated only a slight change from the current distribution, the movement in each category is statistically significant at $\alpha = .05$. Thus, the CPAs anticipated a statistically significant trend toward upgraded services within the next year.

Their predictions by firm size and region are presented in figures 3.8 and 3.9 respectively. No data are presented by city size because there were no statistically significant differences.

A comparison of current and projected distributions reveals that CPAs expected a shift away from compilation toward some form of assurance.

Figure 3.7
CPA Questionnaire
Distribution of Services for Previously Unaudited Clients

	Current Distribution	Projected Distribution
Audits	12.5%	13.8%
Reviews	28.2%	31.5%
Compilations	59.3%	54.7%

Figure 3.8
CPA Predictions
Shift From Unaudited Services to Compilation, Review, or Audit
Disclosure by Firm Size

	Responses	To Audit	To Review	To Compilation
National firms	12	24.5%	41.7%	33.8%
Local firms	33	9.9%	27.8%	62.3%
Probability (p)		.10	.14	.01*

*Differences are significant at $\alpha = .05$.

Figure 3.9
CPA Predictions
Shift From Unaudited Services to Compilation, Review, or Audit
Disclosure by Region

	Responses	To Audit	To Review	To Compilation
Northeast	7	8.6%	55.7%	35.7%
Southeast	12	22.1%	26.4%	51.5%
Midwest	12	10.2%	13.0%	76.8%
Far West	14	12.5%	39.6%	47.9%
Probability (p)		.40	.00*	.03*

*Differences are significant at $\alpha = .05$.

These results should prove encouraging to the banking community, who, according to one executive, "would prefer that accountants attempt to upgrade the service provided—from compilation to review and then from review to audit."[5]

Factors Influencing the Selection of Services

All CPAs participating in this study, both office executives and line individuals, were asked about the comparative influence that certain key factors would have on their recommendations for services in various

---

5. Waterston, "A Banker's Perspective," p. 16.

circumstances. The CPAs were presented with three circumstances:

- A continuing client is considering changing from an audit to a review.

- A prospective client is seeking a compilation or review.

- A continuing client is choosing between a compilation and a review.

The selection of factors included in the study proceeded through several phases. Initially, we generated a list of potential factors that appeared to be relevant to the selection of services in the three hypothetical situations. We then discussed these factors with executives from various CPA firms, and appropriate changes were made. The resulting list served as the basis for the pilot test. Upon completion of the pilot test, participants were asked for verbal comments and suggestions; the factors were then reevaluated, and, where necessary, adjustments were made.

The final factors included in this study fall into three major categories:

- Those related to the client's operations and system (for example, annual revenues and adequacy of internal controls).

- Those related to the accounting firm's perspective (for example, relative fees and the firm's attitude toward compilation and review).

- Those related to the individual CPA's perspective (such as the individual's attitude toward compilation and review).

Continuing Client Considering Changing From an Audit to a Review

The CPA questionnaire presented participants with the following situation:

> For many years your firm has audited the financial statements of Scott, Inc., a family held business which manufactures toys and games.
> The audit service has been performed as a requirement of the loan agreement with the Holder National Bank. At the company's request the lender is considering changing its requirements to allow a review in accordance with SSARS 1. The lender has asked for your advice. Please rank the following 11 factors as to their relative influence on your recommendation. The most important factor should be assigned a rank of 1. Please rank all factors.
> Your responses should reflect your opinion, rather than firm policy.

Figure 3.10 lists the eleven factors and their relative rankings in the aggregate, by size of CPA firm, by size of city, and by region. For each factor, in each context, we computed an arithmetic average of all ranks assigned by the respondents. The factor with the highest rank was assigned a rank of 1, the one with the lowest a rank of 11, and so on. Kendall's coefficient of concordance (W), a nonparametric measure of consensus, is also presented for both the aggregate rankings and the individual breakdowns. This measure, which can range from 0 to 1.0, is statistically significant in each case at $\alpha = .05$. Factors are listed in descending order of importance, based upon aggregate ranking.

Figure 3.10 clearly shows that, in the aggregate and throughout all categories, prior audit experience with the client and adequacy of internal controls are the most influential factors. The individual CPA's attitude and perception of the firm's attitude toward review engagements in general are least important. Clearly, CPAs make such decisions on a case-by-case basis and not on the basis of any overall firm or individual attitude toward the respective services.

Because the fees for a review are substantially less than those for an audit, it is particularly interesting that CPAs do not place much emphasis on comparative fees in assessing the decision to change from an audit to a review.

The results suggest that CPAs are heavily influenced by any prior audit experience with the client, as well as the adequacy of the client's internal controls, in forming a recommendation.

Prospective Client Seeking a Compilation or Review

The CPAs were also presented with the following situation concerning a prospective client for accounting services:

> The Lisa Company, a prospective client, recently contacted you concerning the performance of unaudited accounting services. The Lisa Company is a manufacturer of home furnishings. The firm is family owned and has no significant need for an audit, and has had no prior association with a CPA firm.
> The client has asked you for your recommendation as to which level of service, compilation with or without disclosures, or review, should be performed. Please rank the following 11 factors as to their influence on your recommendation. The most important factor should be assigned a rank of 1. Please rank all factors. Your response should reflect your opinion rather than firm policy.

Figure 3.11 lists the eleven factors and their relative rankings in the aggregate, by size of CPA firm, by size of city, and by region. Again, the W-statistic, computed for each grouping, is significant at $\alpha = .05$.

In this situation, the perceived needs of outside users have the greatest influence on the CPA's recommendation for a compilation or review. One study participant offered the comment, "[The] client should always choose minimum service that meets his company's needs which may include lenders, vendors, customers, majority and minority shareholders, employees' benefit plans, management report(s), internal control review, or whatever other special situations may dictate." Internal control considerations are also extremely important, and, once again, general attitudes are comparatively insignificant; these results are consistent with

Figure 3.10
CPA Questionnaire
Ranking of Factors: Possible Change From Audit to Review

Factors	Aggregate*	Firm Size		City Size		Region			
		Nat'l Firm	Local Firm	Large City	Small City	North-east	South-east	Mid-west	Far West
Prior audit experience with this client	1	1	2	1	2	1	2	2	1
Adequacy of client's internal controls	1	2	1	2	1	2	1	1	2
Your expectations regarding client's future development	3	3	3	3	3	3	3	3	3
Strength of client's preference for a review	4	4	6	4	5	5	5	6	4
Relative percentage of inventory and receivables to total assets	5	5	7	5	6	4	4	4	7
Client's current capital structure	6	6	4	6	7	7	6	5	5

Risk of legal exposure to your firm	7	7	5	7	4	6	7	7	6
Client's annual revenues	8	9	8	9	8	9	8	8	9
Comparative audit and review service fees	8	8	9	8	9	8	9	9	8
Your attitude toward review engagements in general	10	10	11	10	11	10	10	11	10
Your perception of your firm's attitude toward review engagements in general	11	11	10	11	10	11	11	10	11
	W = .35	W = .37	W = .32	W = .35	W = .34	W = .41	W = .32	W = .40	W = .34

*205 responses received

Figure 3.11
CPA Questionnaire
Ranking of Factors: Prospective Compilation or Review Client

Factors	Aggregate*	Firm Size		City Size		Region			
		Nat'l Firm	Local Firm	Large City	Small City	North-east	South-east	Mid-west	Far West
Perceived needs of outside users	1	1	1	1	1	1	1	1	1
Adequacy of client's internal controls	2	2	2	2	2	2	2	2	3
Client's preference for the level of service	3	3	3	3	3	4	3	3	2
Your expectations regarding client's future development	4	4	4	4	4	3	4	4	4
Relative percentage of inventory and receivables to total assets	5	5	6	5	7	5	6	5	7

Risk of legal exposure to your firm	6	7	5	7	5	5	7	7	5
Client's current capital structure	7	6	7	6	6	7	5	6	6
Comparative compilation and review service fees	8	8	9	8	9	8	8	9	8
Client's annual revenues	9	9	8	9	7	9	8	8	9
Your attitude toward compilation and review in general	10	10	10	10	10	9	11	10	10
Your perception of your firm's attitude toward compilation and review in general	11	11	11	11	11	11	10	11	11
	W = .34	W = .35	W = .33	W = .34	W = .37	W = .34	W = .34	W = .40	W = .34

*205 responses received

Figure 3.12
CPA Questionnaire
Ranking of Factors: Continuing Unaudited Client

Factors	Aggre-gate*	Firm Size		City Size		Region			
		Nat'l Firm	Local Firm	Large City	Small City	North-east	South-east	Mid-west	Far West
Perceived needs of outside users	1	1	1	1	1	2	1	1	1
Prior experience with the client	2	2	3	2	2	1	2	3	2
Adequacy of client's internal controls	3	3	2	3	3	3	3	2	4
Client's preference for the level of service	4	4	4	4	4	5	4	4	3
Your expectations regarding client's future development	5	5	5	5	5	4	5	5	5
Relative percentage of inventory and receivables to total assets	6	6	7	6	8	6	7	6	7

38

Risk of legal exposure to your firm	7	7	6	8	6	7	8	8	6
Client's current capital structure	8	8	8	7	7	10	6	7	8
Comparative compilation and review service fees	9	9	9	9	9	11	9	9	9
Client's annual revenues	10	11	10	10	10	8	10	11	10
Your attitude toward compilation and review in general	11	12	12	10	10	8	10	11	10
Your firm's attitude toward compilation and review in general	12	10	11	12	12	12	12	10	11
	$W = .39$	$W = .39$	$W = .34$	$W = .39$	$W = .40$	$W = .38$	$W = .38$	$W = .38$	$W = .38$

* 205 responses received

39

those for the first hypothetical situation. Once again, comparative fees are relatively insignificant.

Continuing Client Choosing Between a Compilation and a Review

The CPA questionnaire included the following situation involving a continuing unaudited client:

> The Mesh Company has been your client for many years. The company is a manufacturer of marine hardware products. In the past, unaudited statements have been issued.
> The client has asked for your recommendation as to which level of accounting service, compilation with or without disclosures, or review, should be performed. Please rank the following 12 factors as to their influence on your recommendation. The most important factor should be assigned a rank of 1. Please rank all factors. Your response should reflect your opinion rather than firm policy.

Figure 3.12 lists the twelve factors and their relative rankings in the aggregate, by size of CPA firm, by size of city, and by region. The W-statistic, computed for each grouping, is again significant at $\alpha = .05$.

The findings are consistent with those for the other situations. The perceived needs of outside users are crucial to the CPA in his recommendation for the level of accounting services that he considers appropriate for a client. The CPA's prior experience with the client and the adequacy of the client's system of internal control also play dominant roles in the recommendation, whereas the individual's and firm's attitudes toward compilation and review are relatively insignificant.

The most interesting dimensions of the results relate to the end points of the rankings. These are the most and least important factors upon the CPA's recommendation for level of service.

Particularly informative is the fact that CPAs react more to the specific needs of outside users and client operations than to predetermined attitudes. This suggests that the CPA's recommendation can be expected to reflect client-specific needs.

Relative Costs of Compilations, Reviews, and Audits

Probably more press coverage was devoted to the potential cost savings resulting from the adoption of SSARS 1 than to any other aspect of the pronouncement. For example, on May 14, 1979, the *Wall Street Journal* predicted that some companies would move from audits to reviews in order to cut costs.[6] A bank executive warned, "Bankers need to be aware

---

6. *Wall Street Journal*, 14 May 1979.

that pressure may be put on them by customers and their public accountants to substitute reviews of unaudited financial statements for existing complete unqualified audits in an effort to save auditing costs."[7]

Yet, prior to this study, no figures had been collected showing the relative costs of the various reporting services now available.

Potential Client

Participants were presented with the following general case, in which a prospective client inquired about the relative costs of audit and other available services.

> You are currently involved in discussions with a prospective client concerning your engagement as the outside accountant. The company, a manufacturer of small steel products, has been averaging $5 million in sales. The company is family owned and is nonpublic.
>
> At present, the discussion centers on the level of accounting or auditing services to be performed. You inform the company that there are four possibilities. Under SSARS 1 a compilation, with or without disclosures, or a review is available as is the traditional audit. The company president has asked the following question:
>
>> Assuming that the hours required for an audit are 100% and that the internal control system is adequate and management is competent, what is the relative percentage of hours required for:
>>
>> a compilation, without disclosures
>> a compilation, with disclosures
>> a review

In the aggregate, the 210 responding CPAs estimated the relative percentages to be as follows: compilation without disclosures, 22.5 percent; compilation with disclosures, 31.9 percent; and a review, 48.9 percent.

These data are disaggregated by firm size, city size, and region in figures 3.13, 3.14, and 3.15 respectively. In the first two breakdowns, the measure of statistical significance is based on the t-statistic, and in the latter, on the F-statistic. Again, a significance level of .05 was used.

It is clear that SSARS 1 requires substantial effort on the part of the CPA for any form of reporting involvement. This conclusion is buttressed by a comment from a study participant who estimated the percent of audit as follows: compilation without disclosure, 25 percent; compilation with disclosure, 50 percent; and a review, 75 percent. The participant explained that his calculation "assumes first time start up cost due to no previous CPA involvement."

Figures 3.13, 3.14, and 3.15 show statistically significant differences in the responses. Local firms and practitioners in small cities are inclined

---

7. Waterston, "A Banker's Perspective," p. 15.

Figure 3.13
CPA Questionnaire
Relative Hours Required for a Prospective Client
Disclosure by Firm Size

	Responses	Compilation Without Disclosures	Compilation With Disclosures	Review
National firms	158	21.3%	30.9%	46.5%
Local firms	52	26.0%	35.0%	56.2%
Probability (p)		.02*	.09	.00*

Note: Audit hours = 100%.
*Differences are statistically significant.

Figure 3.14
CPA Questionnaire
Relative Hours Required for a Prospective Client
Disclosure by City Size

	Responses	Compilation Without Disclosures	Compilation With Disclosures	Review
Large cities	152	21.2%	30.5%	47.5%
Small cities	58	25.8%	35.6%	52.7%
Probability (p)		.04*	.05*	.05*

Note: Audit hours = 100%.
*Differences are statistically significant.

Figure 3.15
CPA Questionnaire
Relative Hours Required for a Prospective Client
Disclosure by Region

	Responses	Compilation Without Disclosures	Compilation With Disclosures	Review
Northeast	52	25.3%	34.5%	51.9%
Southeast	62	23.7%	34.3%	50.1%
Midwest	38	22.4%	32.9%	51.0%
Far West	58	18.7%	26.3%	43.6%
Probability (p)		.05*	.01*	.05*

Note: Audit hours = 100%.
*Differences are statistically significant.

to incur more time for compilation and review services relative to audit time than are their respective counterparts. Also, practitioners in the Far West are likely to incur relatively less time for compilation and review services than are those in other regions.

These results imply that in those cases in which cost is the primary consideration companies in large cities or in the Far West would be more likely to select nonaudit services. Furthermore, because of differences in price structures, firm size may influence the level of service selected.

Continuing Client

Participants were also presented with a case in which a continuing client requested a change to a review.

> For many years your firm has audited the financial statements of A & D Enterprises, a nonpublic manufacturer of small steel products that has been averaging $5 million in annual sales.
> The audit service has been performed as a requirement of the loan agreement with 3rd National Bank. Recently, the lender has indicated a willingness to accept a review in conformity with SSARS 1 instead of an audit. The company president has asked the following question:
> Assuming that the hours required for an audit are 100%, what is the relative percentage of hours required for a review?

In the aggregate, the 210 responding CPAs estimated that a review would cost approximately 43.8 percent as much as an audit.

Figure 3.16 disaggregates these data by firm size and city size. Regional data are not presented because they exhibited no statistically significant differences. The measure of statistical significance is based on the t-statistic at $\alpha = .05$.

Figure 3.16
CPA Questionnaire
Relative Hours Required for a Review of a Continuing Client

Firm Size				City Size		
National	Local	p		Large	Small	p
41.0%	52.4%	.00*		42.2%	47.9%	.04*

Note: Audit hours = 100%.
*Differences are statistically significant.

Recall that, overall, CPAs rank cost considerations as relatively insignificant when recommending a level of service. Because of the substantial cost savings involved in a compilation or review, CPAs will likely face pressure from cost-motivated clients wishing to select one of these services.

Overall Attitudes of CPAs

Attitudes Toward Compilations, Reviews, and Audits

The CPAs were asked to respond to a series of statements expressing attitudes toward various dimensions of the SSARS pronouncements. In each case, they were asked to check one of the following categories to indicate their level of agreement or disagreement with the statement:

Strongly Agree	Mildly Agree	Neutral	Mildly Disagree	Strongly Disagree

The statements can be grouped into the following general categories:

- Minimum level of service appropriate for business clients.
- Reaction to the SSARS pronouncements.
- Legal liability considerations.

A Likert-type, 1-to-5 scale was used to analyze the responses, with 1 meaning "strongly agree" and 5 meaning "strongly disagree." Figure 3.17 lists the mean responses of the 213 respondents. The responses did not differ substantially according to firm size, city size, or region.

Overall, in reference to minimum level of service, respondents felt that compilations without disclosures are generally inappropriate and that compilations with disclosures or reviews should be the minimum acceptable service. One respondent, elaborating in the questionnaire, noted, "Review should be the minimum level of CPA involvement in financial statements to be used outside the client's company. Compilation is useful for internal management purposes." These findings suggest that CPAs will be reluctant to perform compilations without disclosures for externally distributed business financial statements.

Another group of questions relates to the reactions of CPAs to the SSARS pronouncements. The respondents believe that the pronouncements represent a positive move and are expressed clearly. Further, they feel that the proper level of judgment is required. Commenting on the SSARS pronouncements, one study participant stated

SSARS 1 has allowed accountants to more effectively serve the small business concerns at a reasonable fee structure. This has allowed small business to obtain better professional services at costs they can afford as well as better

44

reporting to lending institutions. SSARS No. 1 has provided faster and more communications between small business and lending institutions, especially on reviews and compilations with disclosure.

In addition, participants indicate that they have not encountered substantial implementation problems.[8]

Finally, in regard to relative risk of legal exposure, CPAs perceive that the risk increases as the level of service increases. Dan Goldwasser, an attorney, reached the same conclusion:

> Because of [the review's] novelty, it is not clear which standard of care the courts will apply. One can only imagine that the applicable standard will be higher than that for a compilation engagement but lower than that required for an audit engagement.[9]

He goes on to note that, although SSARS 1 clearly provides benefits to the profession, it exposes the accountant to a greater degree of liability than the unaudited disclaimer.[10]

Attitudes Regarding Personal Financial Statements

Little research has been performed concerning the CPA's association with personal financial statements. To address this issue, we asked the office executives from the national and multioffice local firms and the participating individuals from the single-office firms a series of questions about the number of personal financial statements with which their offices are associated and the current and projected distribution of services.

The fifty-six respondents to this question averaged twelve personal financial statement clients, with a range of none to 100. They estimated the current distribution of services for these clients to have been as follows: audits, 2.6 percent; reviews, 18.2 percent; compilations with disclosures, 47.0 percent; and compilations without disclosures, 29.9 percent. (Because of mathematical errors on the part of the individual participants, the total does not equal 100 percent.) There were no statistically significant differences by firm size, city size, or region.

---

8. This is not to imply that SSARS 1 requires no implementation guidance. See, for instance, John R. Clay, Dan M. Guy, and Dennis R. Meals, *Guide to Compilation and Review Engagements* (Fort Worth, Texas: Practitioners Publishing Company, 1980); John R. Clay, Dan M. Guy, and Dennis R. Meals, "Solving Compilation and Review Practice Problems," *Journal of Accountancy* 150 (September 1980): 74–83; and Larry Perry, "Pitfalls That Practitioners Are Encountering in Compilation and Review Engagements," *Practical Accountant* (December 1980): 17–33.
9. Dan L. Goldwasser, "Liability Exposure in Compilation and Review," *CPA Journal* 50 (September 1980): 29–30.
10. *Ibid.*, p. 31.

Figure 3.17
CPA Questionnaire
Overall Attitudes

Statement	Mean Response
Minimum Level of Service Appropriate for Business Clients	
Compilations without disclosures are inappropriate for business financial statements.	2.5
Compilations with disclosures are inappropriate for business financial statements.	3.8
Nonpublic clients should be encouraged to select review as a minimum level of service.	2.7
Nonpublic clients should be discouraged from changing from audit to review.	3.3
Reaction to the SSARS Pronouncements	
SSARS 1 represents a positive move to expand accounting services to nonpublic companies.	2.4
The SSARS pronouncements create substantial implementation problems.	3.7
The SSARS pronouncements have caused or will cause organizational changes within my firm.	3.7
There are too many specific standards included in the SSARS pronouncements.	3.8
The standards included in the SSARS pronouncements require too much judgment on the part of the accountant.	3.5
The standards included in the SSARS pronouncements are expressed clearly.	2.7
Legal Liability Considerations	
Risk of legal exposure is greater with a review than with a compilation.	2.4
Risk of legal exposure is greater with an audit than with a review.	2.2

The projected distribution in one year was as follows: audits, 2.2 percent; reviews, 21.8 percent; compilations with disclosures, 45.4 percent; and compilations without disclosures, 29.0 percent. (Again, the total falls short of 100 percent.) At $\alpha = .05$, the t-test indicates that the respondents projected a statistically significant movement toward review in one year. No other changes are statistically significant.

The findings demonstrate that less than 25 percent of personal financial statements are likely to be audited or reviewed. The predominant level of service will probably continue to be a compilation.

Summary

This chapter has presented and analyzed the responses of the participating CPAs to the study questionnaire. The CPAs noted a very slight shift from audits to lesser forms of service since the adoption of SSARS 1, and they had similar expectations for the next year. Of their clients who received unaudited disclaimers prior to SSARS 1, approximately 40 percent were now receiving at least some assurance in the form of an audit or review, with little additional change anticipated. The factors most likely to influence the CPA's recommendation for a given level of service relate to the perceived needs of outside users, the client's system of internal control, and any prior experience with the client.

The CPAs estimate that for a prospective client a compilation without disclosures is likely to take between 20 and 25 percent as many hours as an audit, and a review about 50 percent as many hours. The relative number of hours for a review are fewer for a continuing client.

Finally, CPAs believe that a compilation with disclosures or a review is the minimum acceptable service for business clients, and they are generally pleased with the SSARS pronouncements.

4

Study Results—Bankers

SSARS 1 became effective on July 1, 1979. In that month, Edwin A. Schoenborn, then president of Robert Morris Associates, distributed a letter to members concerning this pronouncement. He stated

> The Accounting Policy Committee is of the opinion that pressure may be put on bankers by customers and their public accountants to substitute "reviews" of unaudited financial statements for existing complete unqualified audits in an effort to save auditing costs. Rather than suggesting a downgrading from "audit" to "review," most bankers might rather see an upgrading from "compilation" to "review" and then from "review" to "audit." The degree of assurance resulting from "complete audits" is far greater than that which will result from "reviews." Consequently, you should weigh the cost reduction that your customer could realize from downgrading an "audit" to a "review" against your need to have financial statements with greater reliability and credibility than a "review" statement provides.[1]

The bankers participating in this study were asked to address, among others, the issues raised by Schoenborn. The purpose of this chapter is to present and analyze their responses, which are presented in the aggregate and by city size and region.

The Shift From Audits to Reviews or Compilations

One of the issues raised by Schoenborn relates to the degree of downgrading from audits to lesser services. This section reports on bankers' estimates of any such actual and projected changes.

---

1. Edwin A. Schoenborn, letter to members of Robert Morris Associates, July 1979.

Loan officers participating in the study were asked to indicate the current composition of services for those nonpublic customers that were audited prior to the effective date for SSARS 1. The arithmetic means, based on the responses of 117 bankers, were as follows: audits, 79.2 percent; reviews, 9.3 percent; compilations with disclosures, 4.7 percent; and compilations without disclosures, 5.9 percent. The responses of some individuals did not total 100 percent.

As discussed later in this chapter, there is clear evidence that some bankers have difficulty in differentiating between the various forms of nonaudit reports that they receive. The results do not suggest, however, that they confuse audited and unaudited reports. Therefore, in analyzing data, emphasis should be placed upon the shift from audits to nonaudit services in general. When recast in this manner, the percentages are audits, 79.2 percent, and nonaudit services, 19.9 percent.

It is interesting to compare these findings with the CPA results presented in the preceding chapter. Whereas the bankers estimated a 20 percent downgrade, the CPAs indicated a change of less than 3 percent.

Review of the individual bank questionnaires provides insight into this disparity. A minority of bankers responding to this question, approximately 30 percent, experienced movement away from audits of at least 20 percent of their customers since July 1979; many other bankers encountered only slight movement, and many encountered none.

Thus, our survey indicates that a diverse group of CPAs encountered little downgrading of services and that the majority of an equally diverse group of bankers also encountered little downgrading. The results from the two groups are less discordant than the overall percentages alone indicate; for both groups, only a minority of respondents reported considerable downgrading of services. Also, it must be recalled that the banker and CPA populations did not completely overlap, a fact that complicates any direct comparison between the two sets of results.

We analyzed the questionnaires from individuals reporting downgraded services for at least 20 percent of their customers, looking for differences by city size, region, or bank size, but we found none. Such respondents were spread evenly across all regions and cities, and approximately equal numbers of them were from large as were from small banks. Only one bank (in Atlanta) had a concentration of individuals experiencing such a substantial movement.

The overall responses indicate that there has been some downgrading of services. Although most CPAs have not experienced much downgrading, they can expect more pressure for it as a result of its acceptance by some bankers.

Figures 4.1 and 4.2 present the results by region and city size respectively. Since there is some question about the accuracy of break-

Figure 4.1
Banker Questionnaire
Movement From Audits to Lesser Services
Disclosure by Region

	Responses	Audits	Lesser Services
Northeast	36	84.1%	16.4%
Southeast	37	85.3%	13.1%
Midwest	21	75.1%	26.0%
Far West	23	65.8%	31.3%
Probability (p)		.08	NA

Figure 4.2
Banker Questionnaire
Movement From Audits to Lesser Services
Disclosure by City Size

	Responses	Audits	Lesser Services
Large cities	79	80.2%	18.5%
Small cities	38	77.3%	23.2%
Probability (p)		.66	NA

downs of nonaudit services by some bankers, statistical comparisons are made only for the audit category. The measure of statistical significance is based on the t-statistic for figure 4.1 and the F-statistic for figure 4.2. At $\alpha = .05$, neither of the breakdowns is significant.

The loan officers were also asked to project the composition of services in one year for those customers that were providing audited financial statements. On the average, the 112 respondents expected the following: audits, 82.9 percent; reviews, 10.5 percent; compilations with disclosures, 2.1 percent; and compilations without disclosures, 1.4 percent. (The percentages do not equal 100 percent because of individual errors.) If the data are recast in an audit/nonaudit framework, the results are as follows: audits, 82.9 percent, and lesser services, 14.1 percent.

The bankers predicted a substantially larger trend toward downgraded services than did the CPAs (14.1 percent to 2.4 percent respectively). Review of the bank questionnaires indicates that, once again, a minority of bankers account for this difference. Of the 112 respondents, approximately 25 percent predicted a downgrade within one year by at least 20 percent of those nonpublic customers that were currently providing audited financial statements.

No disaggregated data are presented because there were no statistically significant differences by city size or region.

A related question concerns the bankers' willingness to permit existing audit customers to switch to reviews or compilations. On the average, the 121 bankers responding to the question indicated a willingness to permit 16.3 percent of their audit customers to downgrade. In light of the bankers' prediction that 14.1 percent of such movement would occur within one year, it appears that most permissible downgrades in services would occur within the next year. In selected cases, though, the bankers were willing to allow substantially more downgrading than they expected to encounter in the next year.

In summary, most bankers agreed with the CPAs that only slight movement away from audits had occurred and was likely to occur within the next year. Some bankers, however, experienced a significant movement away from audits, and many of them expected more of the same within the next year. Therefore, CPAs must be aware of the willingness of individual loan officers to accept less than an audit and must consider the bankers' views in counseling clients.

The Shift From Unaudited Services to Compilations, Reviews, or Audits

Current Distribution of Services

Loan officers were asked to estimate the composition of services for those customers previously furnishing unaudited financial statements. On the average, the 110 respondents indicated the following composition: audits, 8.4 percent; reviews, 29.7 percent; compilations with disclosures, 24.2 percent; and compilations without disclosures, 28.7 percent.

We anticipated that the audit, review, and compilation categories would not total 100 percent. Bankers receive financial statements that are self-prepared or prepared on bank forms. In addition, some bankers were still receiving unaudited disclaimers.

At a later stage in the questionnaire, bankers were asked the following:

Since July 1979, approximately how many of your customers' financial statements have been:

_____ Compiled

_____ Reviewed

_____ Accompanied by the old, unaudited disclaimer

_____ Audited

The responses to this question, when coupled with the percentage composition question above, provide revealing insights into actual and perceived experience since the adoption of SSARS 1.

In particular, they help to explain why the bankers' figures total less than 100 percent. The responses suggest that the remainder is at least partly explained by the continued receipt of statements with the unaudited disclaimer. For example, one respondent indicated that 12 percent of formerly unaudited customers were submitting financial statements accompanied by compilation, review, or audit reports. In answering the question about statements received since July 1979, that same individual stated that 77 percent of all such statements were accompanied by the unaudited disclaimer. These findings suggest that, at the time of the study, the reporting requirements of SSARS 1 were not always being followed. Further, they imply that these respondents recognize the difference between the unaudited disclaimer and compilation and review reports.

As the responses to the two questions indicate, many bankers are *not* distinguishing between unaudited disclaimers and compilation and review reports. When asked about the current distribution of services for unaudited customers, these bankers responded that compilations, reviews, and audits now account for 100 percent of these customers; however, when asked, they indicated that they were still receiving statements with the unaudited disclaimer. These responses, when considered together, lead to the conclusion that some bankers are not distinguishing between the unaudited disclaimer and compilation and review. A review of the individual questionnaires reveals that in some cases the bankers were mistaking compilations for unaudited disclaimers and that in others they were confusing reviews and disclaimers.

The results do not indicate, however, that bankers are confusing audited statements with any other statements. A study by Libby and Short supports this conclusion.[2]

Bankers' responses to attitude and perception questions, discussed later in this chapter, indicate that bankers think they understand the differences between the unaudited disclaimer, a compilation, and a review. However, the above results imply that in practice some bankers may not be discerning the differences between the various forms of unaudited reports.

One cause of confusion could be that many CPAs are still stamping "unaudited" on compiled or reviewed financial statements. Thomas Kelley noted, "The committee was unwilling to adopt the suggestion by a number of members that the label 'unaudited' on the financial statements

---

2. Robert Libby and Daniel G. Short, "A Review and Test of the Meaning of Audit Reports From the Perspective of Bankers," *Journal of Commercial Bank Lending* 62 (August 1980): 48–62.

Figure 4.3
Banker Questionnaire
Shift From Unaudited Services to Audits and Lesser Services
Disclosure by City Size

	Responses	To Audits	To Lesser Services*
Large cities	69	10.1%	89.9%
Small cities	41	5.7%	94.3%
Probability (p)		.12	NA

*Including, in some cases, self-prepared financial statements and those prepared on bank forms.

Figure 4.4
Banker Questionnaire
Shift From Unaudited Services to Audits and Lesser Services
Disclosure by Region

	Responses	To Audits	To Lesser Services*
Northeast	35	5.6%	94.4%
Southeast	33	14.5%	85.5%
Midwest	20	5.8%	94.2%
Far West	22	6.2%	93.8%
Probability (p)		.10	NA

*Including, in some cases, self-prepared financial statements and those prepared on bank forms.

be continued, but the final SSARS does not preclude a member from doing so."[3] A knowledgeable compilation and review practitioner has commented that in making many speeches on implementing SSARS 1 he has frequently encountered the question, "Can we still use the 'unaudited' stamp?"

Perhaps the use of the term "unaudited" should be prohibited. Users of financial statements would see only the phrase "See Accountant's Compilation (Review) Report" stamped on each page. Bankers would then see a consistent presentation that would help to clarify the changes wrought by SSARS 1.

---

3. Thomas P. Kelley, "Compilation and Review—A Revolution in Practice," *CPA Journal* 49 (April 1979): 22.

Whatever the cause of the confusion, it apparently does exist; therefore, the distribution of services for formerly unaudited customers can be viewed most meaningfully in terms of an audit/nonaudit dichotomy. The bankers, then, reported that 8.4 percent of formerly unaudited customers were receiving audits and 91.6 percent were receiving lesser services.

Disaggregated data by city size and region are presented in figures 4.3 and 4.4 No statistical tests were performed on the lesser-services category because it includes different types of financial statements. The measure of statistical significance for the audit category is based on the t-statistic for figure 4.3 and the F-statistic for figure 4.4. At $\alpha = .05$, there are no statistically significant differences.

Projected Distribution of Services

Loan officers were also asked to predict the composition of financial statements to be submitted to them in the coming year for those customers providing unaudited statements prior to SSARS 1. On the average, the 118 responding bankers predicted the following distribution: audits, 9.2 percent; reviews, 32.2 percent; compilations with disclosures, 23.4 percent; and compilations without disclosures, 26.0 percent. Again, self-prepared financial statements, statements prepared on bank forms, and continued use of the unaudited disclaimer account for the fact that the percentages do not total 100 percent. Once again, the data are more useful if they are rendered in an audit/nonaudit framework, as in figure 4.5. Disaggregated data are not presented because there were no statistically significant differences by city size or region.

Figure 4.5
Banker Questionnaire
Distribution of Services for Previously Unaudited Clients

	Current Distribution	Projected Distribution
Audits	8.4%	9.2%
Nonaudit services	91.6%	90.8%

These results should encourage those bankers who "feel it is more important to upgrade the assurance provided from the unaudited statement of yesterday to the review or audit of today."[4]

---

4. Thomas L. Stitchberry, *Spokesman* (February 1980). Quoted in *Journal of Accountancy* 149 (May 1980): 97.

Factors Influencing the Required Level of Service

To determine the relative importance of key factors that influence bankers in their decisions about the level of service to require, we presented the participants with three situations and a list of potentially relevant factors for each. The participants were asked to rank the relative impact of these factors. The situations, parallel to the ones presented to the CPAs, were as follows:

- A continuing customer wants to change from an audit to a review.

- A prospective customer is seeking the minimum level of reporting service.

- A continuing customer will not be required to undergo an audit.

As in the case of the CPA questionnaire, the list of factors was modified through discussions with bank executives and the pilot test. These factors cover a broad spectrum ranging from general economic and banking conditions to the specifics of the customer's business and loan request.

Continuing Customer Wanting to Change From an Audit to a Review

The questionnaire included the following situation for a continuing customer:

> The Smith Company has been your customer for several years. You are presently negotiating a new loan agreement. One of the factors being discussed is the level of outside accounting or auditing services to be performed. Past agreements have required the performance of an audit. The customer has requested that a review be allowed instead of an audit. You are considering this request.
> Please rank the following 13 items as to their relative importance to your decision. The most important item should be assigned a rank of 1. Please be sure to rank all items.

Figure 4.6 lists the thirteen factors and their relative rankings in the aggregate, by city size, and by region. For each factor, we computed an arithmetic average of all ranks assigned by the respondents. The factor with the highest rank was assigned a rank of 1, the one with the lowest a rank of 13, and so on. Kendall's coefficient of concordance (W) is again presented for all rankings.

Figure 4.6 shows that loan size is the most influential factor. The customer's current capital structure and reputation and the loan officer's relationship with the customer also influence the decision. Relative costs to the customer were consistently of least importance.

The disregard for relative costs had been predicted. One banker had speculated in print, "I do not feel that the banking community will accept the downgrading of financial information from an audit to a review or compilation for cost savings."[5]

The lack of emphasis on relative costs is consistent with the responses of the CPAs. Bankers, however, will probably face pressure from cost-motivated companies to accept downgraded services.

Overall and throughout most categories, the reputation of the CPA firm is not one of the most influential factors. This suggests that bankers care more about their personal experiences with the CPAs than about firm reputation.

Prospective Customer Seeking the Minimum Level of Service

The bankers were also asked to evaluate relevant factors for a prospective borrower who had indicated a preference for the minimum level of services.

> You are presently in negotiations with the King Company, a prospective customer, concerning a loan agreement. One of the factors being discussed is the level of outside accounting or auditing services to be performed. The prospective customer has indicated a preference for the minimum level of accounting services, due to cost considerations.
>
> You are deciding which of the following four types of services to require: (1) compilation without disclosures; (2) compilation with disclosures; (3) review; (4) audit. Please rank the following 13 items as they would impact upon your decision. The most important item should be assigned a rank of 1. Please be sure to rank all items.

Figure 4.7 shows the thirteen factors and their relative rankings in the aggregate, by city size, and by region.

As in the preceding situation, lenders are most influenced by loan size and the customer's capital structure and reputation. In spite of the customer's stated emphasis on cost savings, relative costs are comparatively insignificant. Possibly most interesting are the factors concerning the outside accountant. The bankers noted that the reputation of the current accountant is not among the more important factors and that the customer's willingness to change accountants is least important. These results should mitigate fears that bankers tend to push new customers to the best known CPA firms.

---

5. Stitchberry, p. 97.

Figure 4.6
Banker Questionnaire
Ranking of Factors: Requested Change From Audit to Review

	Aggregate*	City Size		Region			
		Large City	Small City	Northeast	Southeast	Midwest	Far West
Loan size	1	1	1	1	1	1	1
Customer's current capital structure	2	4	2	3	4	3	3
Relationship with the customer	3	2	5	2	3	4	4
Reputation of the customer	4	3	4	4	2	2	6
Nature of the loan (e.g., line of credit, term loan)	5	5	3	6	5	5	2
Customer's size	6	7	6	7	6	8	5
Nature of the customer's business	7	6	9	8	8	6	7

Relative degree of assurance provided by audit and review	8	9	7	9	7	9	8
Reputation of the outside accountant	9	8	10	5	10	10	11
Profitability	10	10	8	10	9	7	9
Current general credit and economic situation	11	11	11	11	12	11	10
Competitive environment for credit	12	12	12	12	11	12	12
Relative costs of the services to the customer	13	13	13	13	13	13	13
	$W = .35$	$W = .33$	$W = .35$	$W = .41$	$W = .30$	$W = .34$	$W = .38$

*134 responses received

Figure 4.7
Banker Questionnaire
Selection of Level of Services
Ranking of Factors: Prospective Customer

	Aggregate*	City Size		Region			
		Large City	Small City	Northeast	Southeast	Midwest	Far West
Loan size	1	1	1	1	1	1	1
Customer's current capital structure	2	2	2	2	3	3	3
Reputation of the customer	3	3	4	3	2	2	6
Nature of the loan (e.g., line of credit, term loan)	4	4	3	5	4	6	2
Customer's size	5	5	6	6	5	4	4
Relative degree of assurance provided by the above four types of service	6	8	5	7	7	5	7
Nature of the customer's business	7	6	7	8	6	7	5

Reputation of the current outside accountant	8	7	9	4	9	9	10
Profitability	9	9	8	9	8	8	8
Current general credit and economic situation	10	10	11	11	10	11	9
Competitive environment for credit	11	11	10	10	11	10	11
Relative costs of the services to the customer	12	13	12	13	12	12	12
Customer's willingness to change accountants	13	12	13	12	13	13	13
	W = .36	W = .37	W = .35	W = .38	W = .32	W = .38	W = .39

*133 responses received

Figure 4.8
Banker Questionnaire
Ranking of Factors: Continuing Unaudited Customer

		City Size		Region			
	Aggregate*	Large City	Small City	Northeast	Southeast	Midwest	Far West
Loan size	1	1	1	1	1	1	1
Relationship with the customer	2	2	4	2	3	4	4
Reputation of the customer	3	3	3	3	2	3	5
Customer's current capital structure	4	4	2	4	4	2	3
Nature of the loan (e.g., line of credit, term loan)	5	5	5	6	5	5	2
Customer's size	6	6	6	7	6	9	6

Relative degree of assurance provided by the above three types of service	7	9	7	9	7	8	7
Nature of the customer's business	8	7	10	8	9	6	9
Reputation of the outside accountant	9	8	9	5	10	11	11
Profitability	10	10	8	10	8	7	8
Current general credit and economic situation	11	11	11	12	11	10	10
Competitive environment for credit	12	12	12	11	12	12	12
Relative costs of the services to the customer	13	13	13	13	12	13	13
	W = .30	W = .30	W = .32	W = .39	W = .28	W = .24	W = .27

*133 responses received

Continuing Customer for Which an Audit Has Not Been Required

The questionnaire included the following situation for a continuing bank customer that had not previously been required to present audited financial statements:

> The Newton Company has been your customer for several years. You are presently in the process of negotiating a new loan agreement. One of the factors being discussed is the level of outside accounting services to be performed. Past agreements have not required the performance of an audit. Thus, you are presently deciding upon the level of accounting services to require: (1) a compilation without disclosures; (2) a compilation with disclosures; (3) a review.
>
> Please rank the following 13 items as to their relative importance to your decision. The most important item should be assigned a rank of 1. Please be sure to rank all items.

Figure 4.8 lists the thirteen factors and their relative rankings in the aggregate, by size of city, and by region.

A comparison of figures 4.7 and 4.8 demonstrates that virtually the same factors influence bankers in requiring a specific level of service for a continuing customer as for a prospective one. The prior relationship with an existing customer is, however, quite important to this decision. These results imply that lenders evaluate a prospective customer in much the same manner as a current customer when determining the level of appropriate service.

Overall, the results from the three situations indicate that such traditional lending factors as loan size, customer's capital structure, and the banker's interaction with the customer dominate the decision about which service is to be required. Bankers are insensitive to cost considerations in reaching this decision.

Lenders' Perceptions of Appropriate Conditions for Compilations, Reviews, and Audits

Loan officers were asked four questions about the appropriate circumstances for a compilation, review, or audit. They were also asked to indicate any formal bank policy concerning the levels of service.

Not all respondents answered these questions. Furthermore, their answers are, by design, unstructured. Therefore, the discussion that follows represents an abstraction of the bankers' views and is not the result of statistical analysis.

Most respondents indicated that their banks have no formal written policy on level of service. Where there is a policy, an audit is typically required for loans above $100,000.

Compilation Without Disclosures

Not surprisingly, compilations without disclosures are most acceptable in support of small loans. Furthermore, this minimum level of accounting service is most likely to be allowed when

- The customer has a solid reputation and a long-standing relationship with the bank.
- The loan is guaranteed by the owner(s).
- Other appropriate guarantees are involved.
- There is a clear source of loan liquidation.

Many bankers indicate that they would rarely, if ever, accept this type of service in support of a loan.

Compilation With Disclosures

In this context, the size of loan relative to the size of the firm is an important consideration. That is, as the loan becomes a larger percent of total capital, bankers are less inclined to accept a compilation in support of it.

Assuming that the loan size condition is satisfied, bankers are more likely to accept a compilation with disclosures when

- The customer has a good reputation.
- The loan is secured by collateral.
- The loan is guaranteed by the owner(s).
- The loan is short term.
- The CPA has a good reputation.

Several respondents noted that they would seldom, if ever, accept a compilation with disclosures in support of a loan. One study participant maintained, "Compilation statements are a disservice to the customer." Another participant noted, "As a policy for myself, I do not accept compilation under anything other than the most extraordinary circumstances from new business prospects, and I accept them from existing customers only when there is a favorable experience factor and moderate borrowing levels vs. capital." These findings are in agreement with the assessment of one lending officer, who has written that the primary use of compilations "should be to provide interim information or, in a very few cases, to support a low complexity loan."[6]

It should be recalled that, in their rankings of key factors, the bankers indicated that the reputation of the CPA firm does not greatly influence their determination of the appropriate level of service. The fact that the CPA's reputation was listed as a condition for the acceptability of a compilation should not be interpreted as inconsistent. Respondents to this question mention CPA firm reputation as merely one factor; furthermore, these individuals represent only a subset of the aggregate group of participants.

Review

The bankers indicated that the necessity of CPA assurance increases with the size of the loan request. A review is more likely to be allowed instead of an audit when

- The customer has a good reputation.
- The loan is secured.
- The loan is short term.
- The firm is profitable.
- The CPA has a good reputation.

Audit

The loan officers indicated that audits would be required for larger loans. The most commonly stated cutoff was $100,000. In addition, it is likely that an audit would be required when

- There are potential problems (for example, cash flow, losses, or changes in financial position).
- Inventory and receivables are important, are questionable, or have been financed.
- An unknown customer is involved.
- The request is for a term loan.

---

6. Stitchberry, p. 98.

On this subject, a study participant noted the following:

> An audit is a prerequisite for either a term loan or a secured transaction. The size of the loan and/or the customer should also enter into the consideration for asking the borrower for an audit. The customer should be counseled, when appropriate, as to the effectiveness of the audit as a management tool.

Overall Attitudes of Bankers

Attitudes Toward Compilations, Reviews, and Audits

The bankers were asked to respond to a series of statements and questions concerning their attitudes and reactions toward compilations, reviews, and audits. The statements and questions can be grouped into three categories:

- The bankers' understanding of, and familiarity with, the various services.

- Influence of selected factors on the required level of service.

- Reaction to compilation and review services.

Figure 4.9
Banker Questionnaire
Understanding of the Various Services

Statement	Mean Response
Compilation requires inquiry and analytical procedures by the accountant.	4.2
A review provides substantially the same level of assurance as does an audit.	4.1
A review provides more assurance than did previously unaudited statements	1.9
Compilation provides more assurance than did previously unaudited statements.	3.8

Because of a lack of substantial differences across categories, the data are considered only in the aggregate.

The questionnaire addressed the bankers' understanding of the various services by presenting them with a series of statements and asking them to indicate their level of agreement by checking one of the following categories:

Strongly Agree	Mildly Agree	Neutral	Mildly Disagree	Strongly Disagree

A Likert-type, 1-to-5 scale was used to analyze the responses, with 1 meaning "strongly agree" and 5 meaning "strongly disagree." Figure 4.9 lists the mean responses of the 136 respondents.

The bankers were also asked a series of questions about their familiarity with the procedures performed in a compilation, review, or audit. They were asked to circle the category that described their level of familiarity:

1	2	3	4	5
Not at all		Somewhat		Very

Figure 4.10 lists the mean responses of the 136 responding bankers.

Figure 4.10
Banker Questionnaire
Familiarity With the Various Services

Question	Mean Response
How familiar are you with the procedures performed by the accountant in providing compilation services?	3.5
How familiar are you with the procedures performed by the accountant in providing review services?	3.5
How familiar are you with the procedures performed by the accountant in providing audit services?	4.3

Figures 4.9 and 4.10 indicate that bankers do understand the relative levels of assurance provided by the various services but, not surprisingly, are more familiar with audits than with the newer services. The results do suggest that they are "somewhat" familiar with compilation and review procedures.

These findings taken alone indicate that bankers basically understand the differences in services and, logically, could recognize each in connection with actual financial statements. As discussed previously, however, there is doubt about whether some bankers do differentiate among the various services. Many confuse compilation or review with the unaudited disclaimer. Further evidence of the lack of understanding of unaudited services is provided by a study conducted by Bainbridge, in which he concludes

> Bankers and CPAs did not share similar views regarding the CPA's responsibility to evaluate his client's internal control system. Although a majority of the CPAs agreed—as SSARS 1 points out—that such an evaluation is not required, a majority of the bankers was of the opinion that such procedures are performed.
> This misunderstanding could persist in spite of the review report.[7]

Bainbridge goes on to suggest that CPAs might consider increasing direct interaction with bankers in order to clarify the actual nature of procedures performed. The results reported in this chapter support Bainbridge's suggestion.

The bankers were also presented with a series of statements concerning the influence of selected factors on the required level of service. Again, they were asked to indicate their level of agreement with each statement.

A Likert-type, 1-to-5 scale was applied to the responses, with 1 meaning "strongly agree" and 5 meaning "strongly disagree." Figure 4.11 lists the mean responses of the 136 respondents.

Figure 4.11
Banker Questionnaire
Influence of Selected Factors on the Required Level of Service

Statement	Mean Response
The level of accounting services is not a factor in the loan decision.	4.6
Your relationship with the accountant is more important than the level of accounting or auditing services.	3.5
The size of the accounting firm will influence me in determining the acceptable level of accounting or auditing services.	3.1
The reputation of the accounting firm will influence me in determining the acceptable level of accounting or auditing services.	2.0
The client's preference will influence me in determining the acceptable level of accounting and auditing services.	3.2

---

7. D. Raymond Bainbridge, "Unaudited Statements—Bankers' and CPAs' Perceptions," *CPA Journal* 49 (December 1979): 17.

The data in figure 4.11 demonstrate overwhelmingly that bankers view the level of service as influential in the loan decision.

Bankers indicate that they are neutral about the size of the CPA firm when they determine the acceptable level of service. They do, however, mildly agree with the statement that the reputation of the CPA firm would be an influence in determining the acceptable level. This, along with previously discussed findings, clearly shows that the reputation of the CPA firm has some influence on the banker's decision to require a particular level of service, although not as much as traditional loan factors, such as loan size. Furthermore, the respondents view the level of service as more important than any previous relationship with the accountant.

The bankers indicate that they are not likely to be influenced by the client's preferences in determining the required level of service.

The bankers were presented with two statements related to their overall reaction to the introduction of compilation and review. The statements and mean responses, based on a Likert-type scale, are shown in figure 4.12. Thus, the respondents tend to feel that the accounting profession acted appropriately in adopting these services and tend to disagree with the statement that their availability will decrease the reliability of financial statements.

Figure 4.12
Banker Questionnaire
Reactions to Compilation and Review

Statement	Mean Response
The accounting profession acted inappropriately in approving compilation and review services.	3.6
The availability of compilation and review services will generally decrease the reliability I can place on financial statements.	3.5

Nonetheless, the accounting profession needs to take additional steps to refine the implementation of the SSARS pronouncements. This view is expressed by one banker participating in the study, who commented, "In my opinion the AICPA has taken a step in the right direction, but the services should be spelled out more fully."

Attitudes Regarding Personal Financial Statements

Each banker was asked, "What level of service is generally acceptable for individual financial statements in support of a loan?" Respondents to this question indicated overwhelmingly that some form of unaudited report is appropriate. More specifically, most stated that a compilation is acceptable, although others stipulated that a review or even an audit may be required for larger loans. These responses parallel those of the CPAs and reinforce the conclusion that there is a market for compilation services in connection with personal financial statements.

Summary

This chapter has presented and analyzed the responses of the bankers participating in this study. Most of the bankers had experienced only slight movement away from audits and expected more of the same. A minority of bankers, however, encountered a substantial amount of change, and a minority predicted a continuation of this trend. Thus, the overall banker responses differed from those of the CPAs.

In reference to formerly unaudited customers, the bankers indicated that more than 8 percent were being audited, with an anticipation of a slight increase within the next year. There is clear evidence that some bankers were still receiving unaudited disclaimers, while others were confusing compilations and reviews with the pre-SSARS 1 disclaimer. This suggests that the accounting profession needs to refine its communication with lending officers.

Traditional lending factors, such as loan size and the customer's capital structure, have the greatest influence on the banker's decision to require a given level of service, and cost considerations are generally least important. In answer to open-ended questions, the bankers indicated that as the loan increases in size the required level of assurance increases commensurately. Some bankers, however, expressed general opposition to compilations for business customers.

5

Summary and Recommendations

The adoption of Statement on Standards for Accounting and Review Services (SSARS) 1 by the accounting profession in December 1978 (effective July 1, 1979) significantly altered the nature of services available to nonpublic companies. Two specific services with descriptive reports—compilation and review of financial statements—replaced a variety of accounting services that resulted in the unaudited disclaimer. These new services provide for different levels of CPA involvement in cases in which an audit is not performed.

The purpose of this research study was to examine the current and potential impact of SSARS 1 on the market for professional services for nonpublic companies.

To provide the most meaningful results, the study was national in scope. A large and small city from each of four regions was included: New York City and Paterson in the Northeast, Atlanta and Charlotte in the Southeast, Kansas City and Topeka/Lawrence in the Midwest, and Los Angeles and Fresno in the Far West. Two hundred thirteen CPAs from seven national CPA firms and thirty-eight local CPA firms returned the study questionnaires, for a response rate of 61 percent; and 138 bankers participated, for a response rate of 58 percent.

The questionnaires focused on a wide variety of key issues related to the impact of SSARS 1 on the practice of accounting for nonpublic companies.

Summary of Findings

The Shift From Audits to Reviews or Compilations

CPAs and bankers participating in this study were asked to indicate the nature of any current and projected shifts away from audits to reviews or compilations for their nonpublic clients. The CPAs stated that only 2.6 percent had switched to reviews or compilations with disclosures, and they projected that an additional 2.4 percent would downgrade in the next year. In the aggregate, the bankers noted a higher trend away from audits: They estimated that approximately 20 percent of their previously audited nonpublic customers were receiving compilations or reviews. Further, they predicted that 14 percent of their current audited customers would downgrade within the next year.

The disparity between CPA and banker results is explained by the responses of a minority of bankers. These individuals encountered and predicted substantial downgrading (20 percent or more), whereas a majority of bankers and virtually all CPAs sampled experienced and projected only a slight amount of downgrading.

These results provide important insight into one of the key questions raised by the adoption of SSARS 1: Would most nonpublic companies abandon the audit in favor of reviews or compilations? Based on the findings of this study, the answer clearly is *no.* An overwhelming majority of nonpublic companies that were audited prior to SSARS 1 continue to be audited.

Shift From Previous Unaudited Services to Compilations, Reviews, or Audits

The study also addressed the nature of the movement from the unaudited disclaimer to currently available services. The CPAs estimated that, of clients previously receiving an unaudited disclaimer, 12.5 percent were receiving audits, 28.2 percent reviews, and 59.3 percent compilations. Over 40 percent of those companies previously receiving disclaimers were receiving some form of assurance. In addition, the CPAs predicted that within a year approximately 5 percent of the companies receiving compilations would change to reviews or audits.

The bankers' responses highlight some of the difficulties inherent in introducing new levels of services. Some CPAs are still providing the unaudited disclaimer, and many bankers confuse a compilation or review report with the unaudited disclaimer. Both findings underscore the fact that the introduction of compilation and review represented a dramatic change in professional practice, and continual monitoring and refinements are necessary.

Because of the confusion on the part of some bankers about the differences between the various nonaudit services, results are best presented in an audit/nonaudit dichotomy. The bankers indicated that 8.4 percent of those customers previously receiving the unaudited disclaimer were being audited. The remaining 91.6 percent were unaudited. Further, they predicted an increase of less than one percent in the number being audited within the next year.

Factors Influencing Selection of Services

Participants were asked to rank the relative influence of various factors on the selection of services in specific situations. The CPAs rank the perceived needs of outside users, the client's system of internal control, and prior experience with the client as the factors most dominant in influencing their recommendation to the client. Of least importance are their personal and firm's biases toward the services. These findings suggest that CPAs are very sensitive to client-specific needs.

Bankers are most influenced by the loan size, as well as such traditional lending factors as customer capital structure. Relative costs of compilations, reviews, and audits are least significant, in spite of substantial cost differences.

Relative Costs of Compilations, Reviews, and Audits

The CPAs were asked to estimate the relative percentage of hours required for reviews, compilations, and audits. The CPAs indicated that for a prospective client a review is likely to take approximately one-half as many hours as an audit, and a compilation at least 20 percent as many hours. Further, for a continuing client, a review is estimated to take about 44 percent as many hours as an audit. Therefore, a review is less costly for a continuing client than for a prospective client.

Lenders' Perceptions of Appropriate Conditions for Compilations, Reviews, and Audits

Bankers were presented with a series of open-ended questions about the appropriate conditions for each service now available. In response, they noted that there is generally no formal bank policy and that the required level of service for business customers increases with the size and complexity of the loan. They indicate that there is clearly a market for each service.

Overall Attitudes of CPAs and Bankers

The overall views of CPAs and bankers toward the services now available were elicited through a series of attitude questions. Their responses clearly indicate that CPAs consider SSARS 1 a positive development for the profession and that they think it allows the appropriate level of judgment by the accountant. Further, they believe that a compilation with disclosures or a review is the minimum level of service necessary for business clients. On the other hand, for personal financial statements most CPAs support the use of a compilation.

Bankers' attitudes toward SSARS 1 closely resemble those of CPAs; that is, they also believe that the introduction of compilation and review represents a positive development by the accounting profession. Like the CPAs, they overwhelmingly support the use of a compilation for personal financial statements.

Implications

Many people had speculated that the adoption of SSARS 1 would lead scores of nonpublic companies to abandon the audit in favor of reviews or compilations. The results of this study do not support that assertion. In fact, it is clear that nonpublic companies, their CPAs, and bankers continue to value an audit, and only in selected instances is a downgrade likely.

Nonetheless, given the willingness of some bankers to accept downgrades, it is probable that on a case-by-case basis CPAs will face pressure in this direction from their nonpublic clients.

Further, since the adoption of SSARS 1, many companies that previously had unaudited financial statements have opted for some form of report assurance (review or audit). The CPAs participating in this study estimate such movement to be approximately 40 percent of previously unaudited clients.

Bankers' responses to the questions concerning unaudited customers reveal that the adoption of SSARS 1 has created some implementation difficulties and that some CPAs were still furnishing the unaudited disclaimer. Since there is a learning period associated with any technical pronouncement, it is likely that this problem will abate over time.

Some bankers confuse the various types of unaudited services currently and previously available. This finding is particularly interesting because bankers' responses to the attitude questions indicate that they think they understand the differences among the services. Therefore, there is a gap between the actual and perceived ability of some bankers to discern between a compilation, a review, and an unaudited disclaimer. Perhaps the primary reason for this confusion is the continued use of the "unaudited" stamp on compiled or reviewed financial statements.

The relative weights assigned to various factors clearly indicate that CPAs are primarily motivated by client-specific needs rather than general biases in recommending a level of service. This implies that their recommendation will be a function of the specific situation. Further, the bankers' rankings demonstrate that the introduction of compilation and review did not change the basic loan decision model; traditional lending factors continue to dominate the decision. Consistently, the relative costs of the various services were least significant.

Given the disparity in the costs of the services, it is probable that cost-motivated customers will pressure their bankers to allow the use of a minimum level of service. This could ultimately increase the relative significance of cost as a factor in the banker's decision about required level of service.

Further, in regard to costs, the fact that CPAs estimate that, for a prospective client, a compilation takes at least 20 percent as many hours as an audit suggests that SSARS 1 requires substantial effort on the part of the CPA for any form of reporting involvement.

Finally, based on the CPAs' estimates of relative hours, a review is more expensive for a prospective than a continuing client. This difference implies start-up costs.

It is apparent that both CPAs and bankers approve of the adoption of SSARS 1 and are likely to support the continued use of compilation and review services. The overall responses by both groups make it clear that there is indeed a market for compilation and review services. Bankers limit the market for compilations to small, simple business loans or loans to individuals. For more complex or larger loans, they seek a review or an audit.

Recommendations

Based upon the findings of this study, we offer the following recommendations:

- The accounting profession should continue to study the levels of service appropriate for nonpublic companies.

- Accountants should make an effort to determine the attitudes of their clients' bankers toward compilations, reviews, and audits.

- The accounting profession should increase CPAs' awareness that use of the unaudited disclaimer for nonpublic companies is prohibited.

- The accounting profession should take steps to ensure that the unaudited disclaimer is no longer used, and corrective action should be taken where appropriate.

- Consideration should be given to prohibiting the use of the "unaudited" stamp on financial statements.

- It is necessary to educate bankers about the differences between the unaudited services currently and previously available.

- Both formal and informal interactions between CPAs and bankers should increase, with both groups sharing their perspectives and expertise.

- Future SSARS pronouncements should be structured in a manner similar to the existing ones.

Future Research

This study raises several issues suggesting future research. We now have estimates of the relative costs of compilations, reviews, and audits. It would be interesting to investigate the relative assurance of these services, both from CPAs' and users' perspectives. Further, the scope of reviews could be compared across firms to determine the degree of uniformity in review examinations. Similarly, the question of whether this scope should be expanded or contracted in certain areas was not addressed by this study but may warrant investigation.

As indicated by the literature and by the responses of CPAs in this study, the introduction of compilation and review services might well have implications for the legal liability of CPAs. Research is clearly needed in this area to evaluate the relative exposure of CPAs and to offer guidance in minimizing their risks.

APPENDIX A

CPA Questionnaire—Office Executives

CALIFORNIA STATE UNIVERSITY • LOS ANGELES

5151 STATE UNIVERSITY DRIVE LOS ANGELES, CALIFORNIA 90032

SCHOOL OF BUSINESS AND ECONOMICS

We are conducting a research project under the sponsorship of the School of Accounting at the University of Southern California and the School of Business and Economics at California State University to study the need for various types of accounting and auditing services. The results of this study should provide useful information to users and preparers of financial statements.

Your firm has agreed to participate in this study and we would appreciate it if you would complete this questionnaire. It has been pre-tested and experience indicates that it will take about thirty minutes to complete.

Your responses will be held in the strictest confidence. All questionnaires are being handled on an anonymous basis and individual responses will not be reported to your firm or in the research findings. We will be glad to furnish you with a summary of the results. If you would like such a summary, please fill out the enclosed postcard and mail it directly to us.

We urge you to complete this questionnaire at your earliest convenience. Please accept our appreciation for your help in completing this study.

Sincerely,

Jerry L. Arnold

Jerry L. Arnold
University of Southern California

Michael A. Diamond

Michael A. Diamond
California State University, Los Angeles

In December, 1978, the American Institute of CPAs adopted Statement on Standards for Accounting and Review Services No. 1 (SSARS No. 1). Effective July, 1979, this statement allows CPAs to perform compilation and review services as well as the audit. This study asks you to answer a number of questions related to these various types of services. Assume all services relate to annual financial statements of non-public business clients.

As noted before, all questionnaires are handled on an anonymous basis and individual responses will not be reported to the firm or in the research findings. There may be others in your firm participating in this study. In order to insure the integrity of the statistical analysis, please complete this questionnaire without discussing it with your colleagues. Your cooperation in this study is greatly appreciated.

I. Please respond to the five independent situations presented below:

1. Prospective client

    You are currently involved in discussions with a prospective client concerning your engagement as the outside accountant. The company, a manufacturer of small steel products, has been averaging $5 million in sales. The company is family owned and is non-public.

    At present, the discussion centers on the level of accounting or auditing services to be performed. You inform the company that there are four possibilities. Under SSARS 1, a compilation, with or without disclosures, or a review is available as is the traditional audit. The company president has asked the following question:

    Assuming that the hours required for an audit are 100% and that the internal control system is adequate and management is competent, what is the relative percentage of hours required for:

    a compilation, without disclosures   _____ %

    a compilation, with disclosures   _____ %

    a review   _____ %

82

2. Continuing client

For many years your firm has audited the financial statements
of A & D Enterprises, a non-public manufacturer of small steel
products that has been averaging $5 million in annual sales.

The audit service has been performed as a requirement of the
loan agreement with 3rd National Bank. Recently, the lender
has indicated a willingness to accept a review in conformity
with SSARS 1 instead of an audit. The company president has
asked the following question:

Assuming that the hours required for an audit are 100%, what
is the relative percentage of hours required for a review?

_____%

3. Continuing client

For many years your firm has audited the financial statements
of Scott, Inc., a family held business which manufactures toys
and games.

The audit service has been performed as a requirement of the
loan agreement with Holder National Bank. At the company's
request the lender is considering changing its requirements
to allow a review in accordance with SSARS 1. The lender has
asked for your advice. Please rank the following 11 factors as
to their relative influence on your recommendation. The most
important factor should be assigned a rank of 1. Please rank
all factors.

Your responses should reflect your opinion, rather than firm
policy

_____Client's annual revenues
_____Client's current capital structure
_____Risk of legal exposure to your firm
_____Relative percentage of inventory and receivables
             to total assets
_____Comparative audit and review service fees
_____Adequacy of the client's internal controls
_____Prior audit experience with this client
_____Your perception of your firm's attitude toward
             review engagements in general
_____Your attitude toward review engagements in general
_____Strength of client's preference for a review
_____Your expectations regarding client's future development

4. Prospective client

The Lisa Company, a prospective client, recently contacted
you concerning the performance of unaudited accounting services. The Lisa Company is a manufacturer of home furnishings.
The firm is family owned and has no significant need for an
audit, and has had no prior association with a CPA firm.

The client has asked you for your recommendation as to which
level of service, compilation with or without disclosures,
or review, should be performed. Please rank the following
11 factors as to their influence on your recommendation.
The most important factor should be assigned a rank of 1.

Please rank all factors. Your response should reflect your opinion rather than firm policy.

_____Client's preference for the level of service

_____Adequacy of client's internal controls

_____Relative percentage of inventory and receivables
　　　　　　　to total assets

_____Client's annual revenues

_____Your attitude toward compilation and review in general

_____Perceived needs of outside users

_____Your perception of your firm's attitude toward com-
　　　　　　　pilation and review in general

_____Risk of legal exposure to your firm

_____Comparative compilation and review service fees

_____Client's current capital structure

_____Your expectations regarding client's future development

5. Continuing client

The Mesh Company has been your client for many years. The
company is a manufacturer of marine hardware products. In the
past, unaudited statements have been issued.

The client has asked for your recommendation as to which level
of accounting service, compilation with or without disclosures,
or review, should be performed. Please rank the following 12
factors as to their influence on your recommendation. The most
important factor should be assigned a rank of 1. Please rank all
factors. Your response should reflect your opinion rather than
firm policy.

_____Relative percentage of inventory and receivables
　　　　　　　to total assets

_____Your firm's attitude toward compilation and review
　　　　　　　in general

_____Client's annual revenues

_____Comparative compilation and review service fees

_____Client's preference for the level of service

_____Client's current capital structure

_____Adequacy of client's internal controls

_____Prior experience with the client

_____Risk of legal exposure to your firm

_____Perceived needs of outside users

_____Your attitude toward compilation and review in general

_____Your expectations regarding client's future development

II. Please respond to each of the following 12 statements by checking the space which best expresses your agreement:

1. Compilations without disclosures are inappropriate for business financial statements.

Strongly Agree	Mildly Agree	Neutral	Mildly Disagree	Strongly Disagree
____	____	____	____	____

2. Compilations with disclosures are inappropriate for business financial statements.

Strongly Agree	Mildly Agree	Neutral	Mildly Disagree	Strongly Disagree
____	____	____	____	____

3. Non-public clients should be discouraged from changing from audit to review.

Strongly Agree	Mildly Agree	Neutral	Mildly Disagree	Strongly Disagree
____	____	____	____	____

4. There are too many specific standards included in the SSARS pronouncements.

Strongly Agree	Mildly Agree	Neutral	Mildly Disagree	Strongly Disagree
____	____	____	____	____

5. SSARS 1 represents a positive move to expand accounting services to non-public companies.

Strongly Agree	Mildly Agree	Neutral	Mildly Disagree	Strongly Disagree
____	____	____	____	____

6. Non-public clients should be encouraged to select review as a minimum level of service.

Strongly Agree	Mildly Agree	Neutral	Mildly Disagree	Strongly Disagree
____	____	____	____	____

7. Risk of legal exposure is greater with a review than with a compilation.

Strongly Agree	Mildly Agree	Neutral	Mildly Disagree	Strongly Disagree
____	____	____	____	____

8. The standards included in the SSARS pronouncements are expressed clearly.

Strongly Agree	Mildly Agree	Neutral	Mildly Disagree	Strongly Disagree
____	____	____	____	____

9. The standards included in the SSARS pronouncements require too much judgment on the part of the accountant.

Strongly Agree	Mildly Agree	Neutral	Mildly Disagree	Strongly Disagree
____	____	____	____	____

10. Risk of legal exposure is greater with an audit than with a review.

Strongly Agree	Mildly Agree	Neutral	Mildly Disagree	Strongly Disagree

11. The SSARS pronouncements have caused or will cause organizational changes within my firm.

Strongly Agree	Mildly Agree	Neutral	Mildly Disagree	Strongly Disagree

12. The SSARS pronouncements create substantial implementation problems.

Strongly Agree	Mildly Agree	Neutral	Mildly Disagree	Strongly Disagree

III. The following questions relate to the engagements for the office:

1. What percentage of your audit clients have changed to a review?

_____ %

2. In addition to the above, what percentage of your audit clients are likely to change to a review in the next year?

_____ %

3. What percentage of your audit clients have changed to a compilation, with disclosures?

_____ %

4. In addition to the above, what percentage of your audit clients are likely to change to a compilation, with disclosures, in the next year?

_____ %

IV. For the purposes of the following two questions, all of your unaudited clients prior to SSARS 1 should be considered as a group. Estimates should be based upon number of clients.

1. At present the services which you perform for this group of clients are distributed as follows:

_____ % compilation

_____ % review

_____ % audit

___100___ % Total

2. One year from now the services which you perform for this group of clients will most likely be distributed as follows:

_____% compilation

_____% review

_____% audit

___100___% Total

V. The following questions relate to personal financial statements:

1. How many personal financial statements is your office associated with?

_____

2. What is the approximate current distribution of accounting services provided to these individuals?

_____% compilation, without disclosures

_____% compilation, with disclosures

_____% review

_____% audit

3. What do you expect to be the distribution of accounting services provided to these individuals one year from now?

_____% compilation, without disclosures

_____% compilation, with disclosures

_____% review

_____% audit

VI. The following questions relate to your office structure:

1. What is the current size of your professional staff?

_____

2. What is the current ratio between the number of audit and accounting services (compilation and review) clients? (e.g., 2 audit: 1 accounting services)

_____ audit: _____ accounting services

VII. BACKGROUND QUESTIONS

1. Age: _____ years

2. Highest level of education:

_____ High School

_____ 2-Years College

_____ 4-Years College

_____ More than 4-Years College

3. Are you a member of:

_____ AICPA

_____ State Society of CPA's

4. Approximately how many business clients are you responsible for?

_____ less than 5

_____ between 6 and 10

_____ between 11 and 15

_____ between 16 and 20

_____ more than 20. If so, how many? _____

5. Approximate number of years in public accounting:

_____ years

6. Functional responsibility in the firm:

_____

7. Approximately what percentage of your clients receive accounting services instead of an audit?

_____%

8. How familiar are you with the SSARS pronouncements? (Circle one)

<u>1</u>	<u>2</u>	<u>3</u>	<u>4</u>	<u>5</u>
Not at all		Somewhat		Very

9. Approximate time to complete this questionnaire:

_____ minutes

10. Do you have any other comments about this study?

Thank you for completing this questionnaire. Please return the questionnaire directly to us in the attached self-addressed, stamped envelope.

If you would like a summary of the results, please return the self-addressed postcard directly to us. Do not include the postcard with the questionnaire in order to insure the confidentiality of your responses.

CPA Questionnaire—Line Individuals

CALIFORNIA STATE UNIVERSITY · LOS ANGELES

5151 STATE UNIVERSITY DRIVE LOS ANGELES, CALIFORNIA 90032

SCHOOL OF BUSINESS AND ECONOMICS

We are conducting a research project under the sponsorship of the School of Accounting at the University of Southern California and the School of Business and Economics at California State University to study the need for various types of accounting and auditing services. The results of this study should provide useful information to users and preparers of financial statements.

Your firm has agreed to participate in this study and we would appreciate it if you would complete this questionnaire. It has been pre-tested and experience indicates that it will take about thirty minutes to complete.

Your responses will be held in the strictest confidence. All questionnaires are being handled on an anonymous basis and individual responses will not be reported to your firm or in the research findings. We will be glad to furnish you with a summary of the results. If you would like such a summary, please fill out the enclosed postcard and mail it directly to us.

We urge you to complete this questionnaire at your earliest convenience. Please accept our appreciation for your help in completing this study.

Sincerely,

Jerry L. Arnold

Jerry L. Arnold
University of Southern California

Michael A. Diamond

Michael A. Diamond
California State University, Los Angeles

INTRODUCTION

In December, 1978, the American Institute of CPAs adopted Statement on Standards for Accounting and Review Services No. 1 (SSARS No. 1). Effective July, 1979, this statement allows CPAs to perform compilation and review services as well as the audit. This study asks you to answer a number of questions related to these various types of services. Assume all services relate to annual financial statements of non-public business clients.

As noted before, all questionnaires are handled on an anonymous basis and individual responses will not be reported to the firm or in the research findings. There may be others in your firm participating in this study. In order to insure the integrity of the statistical analysis, please complete this questionnaire without discussing it with your colleagues. Your cooperation in this study is greatly appreciated.

I. Please respond to the five independent situations presented below:

    1. Prospective client

        You are currently involved in discussions with a prospective client concerning your engagement as the outside accountant. The company, a manufacturer of small steel products, has been averaging $5 million in sales. The company is family owned and is non-public.

        At present, the discussion centers on the level of accounting or auditing services to be performed. You inform the company that there are four possibilities. Under SSARS 1, a compilation, with or without disclosures, or a review is available as is the traditional audit. The company president has asked the following question:

        Assuming that the hours required for an audit are 100% and that the internal control system is adequate and management is competent, what is the relative percentage of hours required for:

            a compilation, without disclosures   _____ %

            a compilation, with disclosures   _____ %

            a review   _____ %

92

2. Continuing client

For many years your firm has audited the financial statements
of A & D Enterprises, a non-public manufacturer of small steel
products that has been averaging $5 million in annual sales.

The audit service has been performed as a requirement of the
loan agreement with 3rd National Bank. Recently, the lender
has indicated a willingness to accept a review in conformity
with SSARS 1 instead of an audit. The company president has
asked the following question:

Assuming that the hours required for an audit are 100%, what
is the relative percentage of hours required for a review?

_____%

3. Continuing client

For many years your firm has audited the financial statements
of Scott, Inc., a family held business which manufactures toys
and games.

The audit service has been performed as a requirement of the
loan agreement with Holder National Bank. At the company's
request the lender is considering changing its requirements
to allow a review in accordance with SSARS 1. The lender has
asked for your advice. Please rank the following 11 factors as
to their relative influence on your recommendation. The most
important factor should be assigned a rank of 1. Please rank
all factors.

Your responses should reflect your opinion, rather than firm
policy

_____Client's annual revenues
_____Client's current capital structure
_____Risk of legal exposure to your firm
_____Relative percentage of inventory and receivables
              to total assets
_____Comparative audit and review service fees
_____Adequacy of the client's internal controls
_____Prior audit experience with this client
_____Your perception of your firm's attitude toward
              review engagements in general
_____Your attitude toward review engagements in general
_____Strength of client's preference for a review
_____Your expectations regarding client's future development

4. Prospective client

The Lisa Company, a prospective client, recently contacted
you concerning the performance of unaudited accounting services. The Lisa Company is a manufacturer of home furnishings.
The firm is family owned and has no significant need for an
audit, and has had no prior association with a CPA firm.

The client has asked you for your recommendation as to which
level of service, compilation with or without disclosures,
or review, should be performed. Please rank the following
11 factors as to their influence on your recommendation.
The most important factor should be assigned a rank of 1.

Please rank all factors. Your response should reflect your opinion rather than firm policy.

_____Client's preference for the level of service

_____Adequacy of client's internal controls

_____Relative percentage of inventory and receivables to total assets

_____Client's annual revenues

_____Your attitude toward compilation and review in general

_____Perceived needs of outside users

_____Your perception of your firm's attitude toward compilation and review in general

_____Risk of legal exposure to your firm

_____Comparative compilation and review service fees

_____Client's current capital structure

_____Your expectations regarding client's future development

5. Continuing client

The Mesh Company has been your client for many years. The company is a manufacturer of marine hardware products. In the past, unaudited statements have been issued.

The client has asked for your recommendation as to which level of accounting service, compilation with or without disclosures, or review, should be performed. Please rank the following 12 factors as to their influence on your recommendation. The most important factor should be assigned a rank of 1. Please rank all factors. Your response should reflect your opinion rather than firm policy.

_____Relative percentage of inventory and receivables to total assets

_____Your firm's attitude toward compilation and review in general

_____Client's annual revenues

_____Comparative compilation and review service fees

_____Client's preference for the level of service

_____Client's current capital structure

_____Adequacy of client's internal controls

_____Prior experience with the client

_____Risk of legal exposure to your firm

_____Perceived needs of outside users

_____Your attitude toward compilation and review in general

_____Your expectations regarding client's future development

94

II. Please respond to each of the following 12 statements by checking the space which best expresses your agreement:

1. Compilations without disclosures are inappropriate for business financial statements.

_____	_____	_____	_____	_____
Strongly Agree	Mildly Agree	Neutral	Mildly Disagree	Strongly Disagree

2. Compilations with disclosures are inappropriate for business financial statements.

_____	_____	_____	_____	_____
Strongly Agree	Mildly Agree	Neutral	Mildly Disagree	Strongly Disagree

3. Non-public clients should be discouraged from changing from audit to review.

_____	_____	_____	_____	_____
Strongly Agree	Mildly Agree	Neutral	Mildly Disagree	Strongly Disagree

4. There are too many specific standards included in the SSARS pronouncements.

_____	_____	_____	_____	_____
Strongly Agree	Mildly Agree	Neutral	Mildly Disagree	Strongly Disagree

5. SSARS 1 represents a positive move to expand accounting services to non-public companies.

_____	_____	_____	_____	_____
Strongly Agree	Mildly Agree	Neutral	Mildly Disagree	Strongly Disagree

6. Non-public clients should be encouraged to select review as a minimum level of service.

_____	_____	_____	_____	_____
Strongly Agree	Mildly Agree	Neutral	Mildly Disagree	Strongly Disagree

7. Risk of legal exposure is greater with a review than with a compilation.

_____	_____	_____	_____	_____
Strongly Agree	Mildly Agree	Neutral	Mildly Disagree	Strongly Disagree

8. The standards included in the SSARS pronouncements are expressed clearly.

_____	_____	_____	_____	_____
Strongly Agree	Mildly Agree	Neutral	Mildly Disagree	Strongly Disagree

9. The standards included in the SSARS pronouncements require too much judgment on the part of the accountant.

_____	_____	_____	_____	_____
Strongly Agree	Mildly Agree	Neutral	Mildly Disagree	Strongly Disagree

10. Risk of legal exposure is greater with an audit than with a review.

Strongly Agree	Mildly Agree	Neutral	Mildly Disagree	Strongly Disagree

11. The SSARS pronouncements have caused or will cause organizational changes within my firm.

Strongly Agree	Mildly Agree	Neutral	Mildly Disagree	Strongly Disagree

12. The SSARS pronouncements create substantial implementation problems.

Strongly Agree	Mildly Agree	Neutral	Mildly Disagree	Strongly Disagree

III. BACKGROUND QUESTIONS

1. Age: _____ years

2. Highest level of education:

   _____ High School

   _____ 2-Years College

   _____ 4-Years College

   _____ More than 4-Years College

3. Are you a member of:

   _____ AICPA

   _____ State Society of CPA's

4. Approximately how many business clients are you responsible for?

   _____ less than 5

   _____ between 6 and 10

   _____ between 11 and 15

   _____ between 16 and 20

   _____ more than 20. If so, how many? _____

5. Approximate number of years in public accounting:

   _____ years

6. Functional responsibility in the firm:

   _____

7. Approximately what percentage of your clients receive accounting services instead of an audit?

   _____ %

8. How familiar are you with the SSARS pronouncements? (Circle one)

       1   2   3   4   5

       Not   Somewhat   Very
       at
       all

9. Approximate time to complete this questionnaire:

            _____ minutes

10. Do you have any other comments about this study?

Thank you for completing this questionnaire. Please return the questionnaire directly to us in the attached self-addressed, stamped envelope.

If you would like a summary of the results, please return the self-addressed postcard directly to us. Do not include the postcard with the questionnaire in order to insure the confidentiality of your responses.

APPENDIX C

Banker Questionnaire

CALIFORNIA STATE UNIVERSITY • LOS ANGELES

5151 STATE UNIVERSITY DRIVE LOS ANGELES, CALIFORNIA 90032

SCHOOL OF BUSINESS AND ECONOMICS

We are conducting a research project under the sponsorship of the School of Business and Economics at California State University, Los Angeles, and the School of Accounting at the University of Southern California to study the need for various types of accounting and auditing services. The results of this study should provide useful information to users and preparers of financial statements.

Your bank has agreed to participate in this study and we would appreciate it if you would complete this questionnaire. It has been pre-tested and experience indicates that it will take about thirty minutes to complete.

Your responses will be held in the strictest confidence. All questionnaires are being handled on an anonymous basis and individual responses will not be reported to the bank or in the research findings. We will be glad to furnish you with a summary of the results. If you would like such a summary, please fill out the enclosed postcard and mail it directly to us.

We urge you to complete this questionnaire at your earliest convenience. Please accept our appreciation for your help in completing this study.

Sincerely,

Jerry L. Arnold

Jerry L. Arnold
University of Southern California

Michael A. Diamond

Michael A. Diamond
California State University, Los Angeles

INTRODUCTION

In December, 1978, the American Institute of CPAs adopted a <u>Statement</u> <u>on Standards for Accounting and Review Service</u> No. 1 (SSARS No. 1). Effective July, 1979, this statement allows CPAs to perform compilation and review services as well as the independent audit. This study asks you to answer a number of questions related to these various types of services.

We recognize that you are being asked to answer questions based upon a subset of the information that you might normally consider. Please remember that we are not testing your abilities as a loan officer; we are studying the relationship between accounting services and bank loan decisions for non-public customers. As noted before, all questionnaires are handled on an anonymous basis and individual responses will not be reported to the bank or in the research findings.

Finally, there may be others in your bank participating in this study. In order to insure the integrity of the statistical analysis please complete this questionnaire without discussing it with your colleagues. Your cooperation in this study is greatly appreciated.

I. In responding to the three situations presented below, please assume that:

  (1) All other financial and non-financial loan conditions normally considered have been met to your bank's satisfaction.

  (2) Your bank has adequate funds available to make the required loans.

  (3) Each company is <u>non-public</u>.

  1. Continuing customer

    The Smith Company has been your customer for several years. You are presently negotiating a new loan agreement. One of the factors being discussed is the level of outside accounting or auditing services to be performed. Past agreements have required the performance of an audit. The customer has requested that a review be allowed instead of an audit. You are considering this request.

    Please rank the following 13 items as to their relative importance to your decision. The most important item should be assigned a rank of 1. Please be sure to rank all items.

    _____ Loan size

    _____ Customer's size

    _____ Nature of the loan (e.g., line of credit, term loan)

    _____ Customer's current capital structure

    _____ Reputation of the outside accountant

_____ Competitive environment for credit

_____ Nature of the customer's business

_____ Relationship with the customer

_____ Current general credit and economic situation

_____ Relative costs of the services to the customer

_____ Relative degree of assurance provided by audit and review

_____ Reputation of the customer

_____ Profitability

2. Prospective customer

You are presently in negotiations with the King Company, a prospective customer, concerning a loan agreement. One of the factors
being discussed is the level of outside accounting or auditing
services to be performed. The prospective customer has indicated
a preference for the minimum level of accounting services, due to
cost considerations.

You are deciding which of the following four types of services to
require: (1) compilation without disclosures; (2) compilation with
disclosures; (3) review; (4) audit. Please rank the following 13
items as they would impact upon your decision. The most important
item should be assigned a rank of 1. Please be sure to rank all
items.

_____ Customer's size

_____ Customer's current capital structure

_____ Customer's willingness to change accountants

_____ Nature of the customer's business

_____ Relative costs of the services to the customer

_____ Profitability

_____ Loan size

_____ Nature of the loan (e.g., line of credit, term loan)

_____ Reputation of the current outside accountant

_____ Competitive environment for credit

_____ Current general credit and economic situation

_____ Relative degree of assurance provided by the above
          four types of services

_____ Reputation of the customer

3. Continuing customer

The Newton Company has been your customer for several years. You are presently in the process of negotiating a new loan agreement. One of the factors being discussed is the level of outside accounting services to be performed. Past agreements have not required the performance of an audit. Thus, you are presently deciding upon the level of accounting services to require: (1) a compilation without disclosures; (2) a compilation with disclosures; (3) a review.

Please rank the following 13 items as to their relative importance to your decision. The most important item should be assigned a rank of 1. Please be sure to rank all items.

_____ Relative costs of the services to the customer

_____ Relationship with the customer

_____ Competitive environment for credit

_____ Customer's current capital structure

_____ Customer's size

_____ Reputation of customer

_____ Current general credit and economic situation

_____ Nature of the customer's business

_____ Reputation of the outside accountant

_____ Nature of the loan (e.g., line of credit, term loan)

_____ Loan size

_____ Profitability

_____ Relative degree of assurance provided by the above three types of services

II. The following questions relate to those customers for which you are responsible. Estimates should be based on number of customers.

1. What percentage of your customers that <u>previously</u> provided you with AUDITED financial statements now provide you with:

    compilation statements, without disclosures _____ %

    compilation statements, with disclosures _____ %

    review statements _____ %

    audited statements _____ %

2. What percentage of your customers that <u>currently</u> provide you with AUDITED financial statements would you <u>permit</u> to switch to:

    compilation statements, without disclosures _____ %

    compilation statements, with disclosures _____ %

    review statements _____ %

104

3. One year from now, what percentage of your customers that <u>currently</u> provide you with AUDITED financial statements do you expect to provide you with:

compilation statements, without disclosures _____%

compilation statements, with disclosures _____%

review statements _____%

audited statements _____%

4. What percentage of your customers that <u>previously</u> provided you with UNAUDITED financial statements now provide you with:

compilation statements, without disclosures _____%

compilation statements, with disclosures _____%

review statements _____%

audited statements _____%

5. One year from now, what percentage of your customers that <u>previously</u> provided you with UNAUDITED statements do you expect will provide you with:

compilation statements, without disclosures _____%

compilation statements, with disclosures _____%

review statements _____%

audited statements _____%

6. Under which circumstances would you insist upon an audit in support of a loan?

III. Please respond to each of the following 11 statements by checking the space which best expresses your level of agreement:

1. Compilation requires inquiry and analytical procedures by the accountant.

Stongly Agree	Mildly Agree	Neutral	Mildly Disagree	Strongly Disagree

2. A review provides substantially the same level of assurance as does an audit.

Strongly Agree	Mildly Agree	Neutral	Mildly Disagree	Strongly Disagree

3. The level of accounting services is not a factor in the loan decision.

Strongly Agree	Mildly Agree	Neutral	Mildly Disagree	Strongly Disagree

4. A review provides more assurance than did previously unaudited
   statements.

   | Strongly | Mildly | Neutral | Mildly | Strongly |
   | Agree | Agree | | Disagree | Disagree |

5. Compilation provides more assurance than did previously unaudited
   statements.

   | Strongly | Mildly | Neutral | Mildly | Strongly |
   | Agree | Agree | | Disagree | Disagree |

6. The accounting profession acted inappropriately in approving
   compilation and review services.

   | Strongly | Mildly | Neutral | Mildly | Strongly |
   | Agree | Agree | | Disagree | Disagree |

7. Your relationship with the accountant is more important than
   the level of accounting or auditing services.

   | Strongly | Mildly | Neutral | Mildly | Strongly |
   | Agree | Agree | | Disagree | Disagree |

8. The availability of compilation and review services will generally
   decrease the reliability I can place on financial statements.

   | Strongly | Mildly | Neutral | Mildly | Strongly |
   | Agree | Agree | | Disagree | Disagree |

9. The size of the accounting firm will influence me in determining
   the acceptable level of accounting or auditing services.

   | Strongly | Mildly | Neutral | Mildly | Strongly |
   | Agree | Agree | | Disagree | Disagree |

10. The reputation of the accounting firm will influence me in determining
    the acceptable level of accounting or auditing services.

    | Strongly | Mildly | Neutral | Mildly | Strongly |
    | Agree | Agree | | Disagree | Disagree |

11. The client's preference will influence me in determining the accept-
    able level of accounting and auditing services.

    | Strongly | Mildly | Neutral | Mildly | Strongly |
    | Agree | Agree | | Disagree | Disagree |

IV. The following questions relate to your acceptance of and experience
    with various accounting and auditing services:

    1. How familiar are you with the procedures performed by the
       accountant in providing compilation services? (Circle one)

       | 1 | 2 | 3 | 4 | 5 |
       | Not | | Somewhat | | Very |
       | at | | | | |
       | all | | | | |

2. How familiar are you with the procedures performed by the accountant in providing review services? (Circle one)

   <u>1</u>   <u>2</u>   <u>3</u>   <u>4</u>   <u>5</u>

   Not   Somewhat   Very
   at
   all

3. How familiar are you with the procedures performed by the accountant in providing audit services? (Circle one)

   <u>1</u>   <u>2</u>   <u>3</u>   <u>4</u>   <u>5</u>

   Not   Somewhat   Very
   at
   all

4. Under which circumstances would you accept compilation services, without disclosures, in support of a loan?

5. Under which circumstances would you accept compilation services, with disclosures, in support of a loan?

6. Under which circumstances would you accept review services in support of a loan?

7. What level of service is generally acceptable for individual financial statements in support of a loan?

8. Since July, 1979, approximately how many of your customers' financial statements have been:

   _____ compiled

   _____ reviewed

   _____ accompanied by the old, unaudited disclaimer

   _____ audited

9. Briefly describe your bank's formal policy, if any, concerning required levels of accounting services.

V. BACKGROUND QUESTIONS

1. Age: _____ years

2. Highest level of education:

    _____ Grammar School

    _____ High School

    _____ 2-Years College

    _____ 4-Years College

    _____ More than 4-Years College

3. Approximately how many commercial loan applications have you evaluated during the past year?

    _____ less than 10

    _____ between 11 and 20

    _____ between 21 and 30

    _____ between 31 and 40

    _____ between 41 and 50

    _____ more than 50, how many? _____

4. Which of the following best describes your position within the bank?

    _____ line lending

    _____ manager of lending group

    _____ credit approval and review officer

    _____ loan examiner

5. Approximate number of years employed as a loan officer:

    _____ years

6. Approximately what percentage of your customers are non-public?

    _____ %

7. Approximate time to complete this questionnaire:

    _____ minutes

8. Do you have any other comments about this study?

Thank you for completing this questionnaire. Please return the questionnaire directly to us in the attached self-addressed stamped envelope.

If you would like a summary of the results, please return the self-addressed postcard directly to us. Do not include the postcard with the questionnaire in order to insure the confidentiality of your responses.

Bibliography

American Institute of Certified Public Accountants. Exposure draft of a proposed statement on standards for accounting and review services, *Compilation and Review of Financial Statements.* New York: AICPA, 1978.

American Institute of Certified Public Accountants. *Report, Conclusions, and Recommendations of the Commission on Auditors' Responsibilities.* New York: AICPA, 1978.

American Institute of Certified Public Accountants. *Report of the Committee on Generally Accepted Accounting Principles for Smaller and/or Closely Held Businesses.* New York: AICPA, 1976.

American Institute of Certified Public Accountants. Statement on Auditing Standards 25. *The Relationship of Generally Accepted Auditing Standards to Quality Control Standards.* New York: AICPA, 1979.

American Institute of Certified Public Accountants. Statement on Auditing Standards 1. *Codification of Auditing Standards and Procedures.* New York: AICPA, 1973.

American Institute of Certified Public Accountants. Statement on Standards for Accounting and Review Services 1. *Compilation and Review of Financial Statements.* New York: AICPA, 1978.

American Institute of Certified Public Accountants. Statement on Standards for Accounting and Review Services 2. *Reporting on Comparative Financial Statements.* New York: AICPA, 1979.

American Institute of Certified Public Accountants. Task Force on Unaudited Financial Statements. *Guide for Engagements of CPAs to Prepare Unaudited Financial Statements.* New York: AICPA, 1975.

Bainbridge, D. Raymond. "Unaudited Statements—Bankers' and CPAs' Perceptions." *CPA Journal* 49 (December 1979): 11–17.

Brasseaux, J. H., and Pearl, Daniel. "Reviews and Compilation: An Analysis and Survey of Their Expected Impact." *Louisiana Certified Public Accountant* (Winter/Spring 1979/80): 33–53.

Brown, Harry G. "Compilation and Review—A Step Forward?" *CPA Journal* 49 (May 1979): 18–23.

Chazen, Charles. Reply to John S. Waddell, "Compilation of Financial Statements—A Professional Service." *Journal of Accountancy* 146 (September 1978): 98–99.

Clay, John R.; Guy, Dan M.; and Meals, Dennis R. *Guide to Compilation and Review Engagements*. Fort Worth, Texas: Practitioners Publishing Company, 1980.

Clay, John R.; Guy, Dan M.; and Meals, Dennis R. "Solving Compilation and Review Practice Problems." *Journal of Accountancy* 150 (September 1980): 74–83.

Dirkes, Kenneth J., and Deming, John R. "Audit, Compilation or Review?" *CPA Journal* 50 (April 1980): 85–89.

Financial Accounting Standards Board. "FASB Invitation to Comment on Financial Statements and Other Means of Financial Reporting." Stamford, Connecticut: FASB, May 1980.

Goldwasser, Dan L. "Liability Exposure in Compilation and Review." *CPA Journal* 50 (September 1980): 27–31.

Gregory, William R. "Unaudited but OK?" *Journal of Accountancy* 145 (February 1978): 61–65.

Gregory, William R., and Kelley, Thomas P. "Compilation, Review, and the Division for CPA Firms—Their Impact on the Small Business Customer and His Banker." *Journal of Commercial Bank Lending* 61 (August 1979): 2–10.

Gutberlet, Louis G. "Accounting and Review Services." *Journal of Accounting Auditing and Finance* 4 (Winter 1981): 169–178.

Gutberlet, Louis G. "Compilation and Review of Financial Statements by an Accountant." *Journal of Accounting Auditing and Finance* 3 (Summer 1980): 313–338.

Guy, Dan M., and Tatum, Kay W. "Handling Compilation and Review Engagements: A Step-by-Step Approach." *Practical Accountant* 12 (September 1979): 21–29.

Hubbard, Thomas D., and Lambert, Joyce C. "Current and Proposed Unaudited Statement Standards." *CPA Journal* 48 (August 1978): 35–41.

Kelley, Thomas P. "Compilation and Review—A Revolution In Practice." *CPA Journal* 49 (April 1979): 19–27.

King, Earle V., and Cote, Joseph T. "Compilation and Review." *California CPA Quarterly* 47 (June 1979): 9–14.

Libby, Robert, and Short, Daniel G. "A Review and Test of the Meaning of Audit Reports From the Perspective of Bankers." *Journal of Commercial Bank Lending* 62 (August 1980): 48–62.

Miller, Robert D. "Accounting and Review Services—Background and Concepts." *Connecticut CPA* 43 (March 1980): 6–8.

Munter, Paul, and Ratcliffe, Thomas A. "Nonaudit Engagements." *CPA Journal* 50 (July 1980): 74–77.

Perry, Larry. "Pitfalls That Practitioners Are Encountering in Compilation and Review Engagements." *Practical Accountant* (December 1980): 17–33.

Ratcliffe, Thomas A., and Munter, Paul. "Reporting on Comparative Financial Statements: SSARS 2." *CPA Journal* 50 (March 1980): 69–72.

Schoenborn, Edwin A. Letter to members of Robert Morris Associates. July 1979.

Stitchberry, Thomas L. *Spokesman* (February 1980). Quoted in *Journal of Accountancy* 149 (May 1980): 97–98.

Waddell, John S. "Compilation of Financial Statements—A Professional Service." *Journal of Accountancy* 146 (September 1978): 95–98.

Wallace, Wanda A. "New AICPA Standards for Smaller Companies." *Bankers Monthly Magazine* 46 (August 1979): 30–31.

Wall Street Journal. 14 May 1979.

Waterston, James R. "Compilation, Review, and the Division for CPA Firms: A Banker's Perspective." *Journal of Commercial Bank Lending* 61 (August 1979): 11–18.

Winters, Alan J. "Banker Perceptions of Unaudited Financial Statements." *CPA Journal* 45 (August 1975): 29–33.

Winters, Alan J. "Unaudited Statements: Review Procedures and Disclosures." *Journal of Accountancy* 142 (July 1976): 52–59.